The Changeling

The Burning of Bridget Cleary

Mary Ann Benbow.

Copyright(©)

Mary Ann Benbow reserves the right to this bool. No part of it can

Reproduced without the written consent of the author.

THE FAERY WIFE

Chapter One.

The Clonmel Witch Burning' (1895)

Nowadays, we tend to think of witchcraft as something that belongs to some distant and more barbarous time—usually the medieval or dark ages—but the last 'witch burning' in the British Isles was much more recent than that. And it happened in Ireland. The burning of Bridget Cleary in Ballyvadlea, near Clonmel in County Tipperary, occurred as recently as 1895 and was widely reported in the newspapers of the day.

The case, which provoked widespread interest at the time (the noted writer, E. F. Benson, author of the celebrated Mapp and Lucinda books, wrote an article on the incident in the highly influential journal The Nineteenth Century), is a curious amalgam of folk-belief, local fears, and fairy lore. A belief in witchcraft, fairy abductions, and malign powers was still deeply rooted in the local mind, and this was to have terrifying and fatal results.

The notion of fairies being involved with alleged witches was not unique to southern Tipperary. Indeed, the two were inextricably linked in many parts of rural Ireland. It was believed that wise women and 'fairy doctors' (rural healers) had received their knowledge and skills from the Little People (fairies) and maintained close links with them.

Changelings

It was also believed that fairies intervened more frequently in human affairs than was commonly supposed. From time to time, it was said, they might even spirit individuals away to live with them for a time and 'teach them things'. In some cases, a representation of the person"—a stock'—might be left in its place to trick the community into believing that the person concerned was still amongst them. Small children and newborn babies were particularly at risk of such abductions until they were baptised, but even adults who had perhaps committed some sin might be 'taken away' as well.

The physical appearance of those who had been 'taken' often changed. This change was apparent in babies and the very young—children who had been healthy-looking the evening before were often found thin, wrinkled, and wasted in the morning. In many cases, the notion of being changed for a stock often helped to explain the sudden onset and effects of infant tuberculosis. At one time, during an epidemic of the disease in the Burren region of County Clare, the physical appearance of the victims was put down to the fact that they'd been stolen by fairies or evil entities.

Adults, too, could be stolen, and a formerly healthy individual could be replaced with a withered, moaning thing. This was a central aspect of the Ballyvadlea witchcraft burning, where the victim was believed to have become possessed by a malevolent fairy or demonic presence.

Superstition and Murder

The incident itself should be seen in the context of a spate of Irish 'changeling' incidents that spanned the nineteenth century. In 1826, The Morning Post reported the following from Tralee Assizes:
"Ann Roche, an old woman of very advanced age, was indicted for the murder of Michael Leahy, a young child, by drowning in the river Flesk. This case turned out to be a homicide committed under the delusion of the grossest superstition. The child, though four years old, could neither stand, walk, nor speak—it was thought to be fairy-struck—and the grandmother ordered the prisoner and one of the witnesses, Mary Clifford, to bathe the child every morning in that pool of the River Flesk where boundaries of three farms met; and on the last morning, the prisoner kept the child under the water longer than usual. Upon cross-examination, the witness said that it was not done with the intent to kill the child but to cure it—to put the fairy out of it.
The court returned a 'not guilty' verdict at the judge's direction, revealing the depth of belief in changelings within the community. Yet the countryside around Glenflesk was not the only region in which such superstitions manifested themselves.

In 1888, Johanna Doyle appeared at Assizes near Killarney on a charge of child murder. She was charged with butchering her own mentally retarded son, Patsy, with a hatchet, assisted by her husband and three of her other children. During her trial, she insisted that thirteen-year-old Patsy had been 'a fairy and a devil', having been 'changed' by the fairies. The family had been dogged by strange events in recent years, and this had been put down to Patsy's influence. Other Incidents Such incidents were not confined to County Kerry. A series of changeling-related incidents occurred in County Tipperary. around the mid-to-late 1800s. There are, for example, several alleged instances around Roscrea in the north of the county that seemingly took place around the 1860s, but no definite information on them has been recorded. But it was in the south of the county that the most serious instances seem to have occurred.

The Daily Telegraph dated 19 May 1884 notes an arrest of two women in Clonmel on the suspicion of having harmed a three-year-old child named Philip Dillon. In court, Anastasia Bourke and Ellen Cushion stated that they believed the child, who didn't have the use of his limbs, to be one of the fairykind left in exchange for the original infant.

While the mother was absent, they entered the house and, seizing the unfortunate child, placed him naked on an iron shovel, holding him over a fire (a common way in rural areas to drive out malign creatures and spirits). They hoped to 'break the charm' and destroy the changeling's powers. The boy was badly burned, and the newspaper reported him to be in a serious condition. The prisoners were remanded in custody to stand trial, but no further account exists. During the hearing, they were hooted and sneered at by locals.

The most notorious case, however, also comes from the Clonmel area and concerns Bridget Cleary, who has been ignominiously dubbed 'Ireland's last witch'. The horrific events that surround her death have been recorded as the 'last witch burning in the British Isles' and have often been cited by English writers as evidence of profound ancient superstition. still existing in the Irish countryside during the late nineteenth century.

Bridget's Local Community

Bridget Cleary was born and died in remote Ballyvadlea, near Clonmel. She was only twenty-six at the time of her death in 1896. According to The Cork Examiner, she was a pretty woman of medium height and had a strong, independent mind. Her parents, Patrick and Bridget Boland, poor Catholic rural labourers, were devoutly religious and extremely superstitious. This was not surprising, considering the area in which they lived.

Ballyvadlea was steeped in folklore and tradition. All through the area, the remnants of ancient earthen forts and tumuli hinted at ancient lore and secrets. From the road running through the district, travellers could see the distant slopes of Slievenamon—the fairy-haunted mountain once said to be the stronghold of the Fenian knights—where all manner of supernatural creatures were said to dwell.

Between its lower slopes and Fethard town, many 'slieveens' lived. They were the 'fairy doctors' or 'cunning men' who were familiar with the ways of the Little People and displayed skills verging on the supernatural. These were men like Denis Ganey, who resided in a thatched cabin on the mountainside, or John (Jack) Dunne, a limping, toothless man who trapped the streets of both Clonmel and Fethard, telling tales of fairies and ghosts.

There were fairy-haunted sites everywhere. At certain times of the year, Slievenamon itself was reputedly frequented by witches and enchanters from all over Ireland. Close to where the Bolands lived rose the brooding bulk of Kylenagranagh Hill, which was topped with a fairy fort or rath—reputedly a 'sheehoguey' place (a site of supernatural dread) where the Sidhe or the fairy host held court and plotted mischief against the humans who lived around them. Local people avoided the place; beliefs connecting such sites with supernatural dangers ran very deep among them.

Although a strong-willed and opinionated young woman, Bridget Boland does not appear to have felt the need to move away from her narrow rural environment. Always good at sewing and stitching, she became a self-employed dressmaker, working from home. Indeed, as her father was to state later, she became one of the first women in Ballyvadlea.

to own a new Singer sewing machine, which she kept in her bedroom.

Her new business venture seems to have been popular throughout the local community, and soon Bridget Boland was relatively prosperous, which added to her desirability amongst the young men in the surrounding townlands of Ballyvadlea, Cloneen, and Mullinahone. She could have had her pick of any of them.

A stylish young woman by all accounts, it appears that she was noticed by one of the local landowners who, on his way to hunt with the Tipperary Hounds, had been so struck by her. attractiveness as she passed him on the road that he had asked who she was and later claimed that the memory of her had stayed with him into old age. Her prettiness had also turned the heads of many of the young labourers in the area. However, the man she chose as her husband came as a surprise to the entire community. He was Michael Cleary, a dark, brooding character, almost ten years older than herself.

Married Life

It is thought that Bridget and Michael met in Clonmel town. He was a dark and sullen man who reputedly had never bothered much with women and was highly superstitious. He was, for example, wary of his wife's mother, Bridget Keating, who had been seen as a 'fairy woman' who had been 'taken' several times.

Michael was an unlikely partner for the independent Bridget. Even so, they were married in August 1887. Bridget was eighteen, nine years younger than Michael, and unusually young to be married. The marriage was even more strange because, for some time after the wedding, Michael continued to live in Clonmel while Bridget returned home every evening to her parents' house near Ballyvadlea Bridge. Perhaps Bridget was needed at home to look after her ill mother (who died around 1893), but there were other rumours too.

Some suggested that Bridget might be seeing someone else, and the consensus was that her neighbour, William Simpson, was the man. If the affair existed (and there's no evidence that it did), there were good reasons for keeping it quiet. Simpson was married and lived with his wife and children in a farmhouse a few hundred yards from the Clearys.

William and his family occupied a farm from which the landlord, his employer, had evicted the previous tenants some years before. But there was something else—the Simpsons were Protestants, and, in a conservatively Catholic area, the idea of a young Catholic girl consorting with a married Protestant was scandalous.

There was probably no truth at all in the rumours, but it fits well with what some locals considered to be Bridget's 'high and mighty' attitude. If the stories about his wife ever reached Michael Cleary in Clonmel, he appeared to take no heed of them.

New Home

A little while after Bridget's marriage, the Cashel Poor Law Guardians erected a new cottage in the district under the 1883 Labourer's (Ireland) Act. Designed to suit a labouring family, it was built about half a mile up the hill from Ballyvadlea Bridge in the townland of Tullowcossaun. From the door and front window, it had a direct view across the countryside to distant Slievenamon.

It was a fine, modern structure with a slanted roof and a chimney at each gable and, as such, was considered much grander than the cabin's roundabout. There was one drawback, however. It had been built on the site of an old fairy rath, and the immediate area was widely regarded as a supernatural site. Such a reputation deterred many locals from applying for its tenancy.

Nevertheless, in the late 1880s, Bridget and Michael Cleary applied for tenancy of the new cottage. They were unsuccessful, and the place was given to another labourer. Shortly after he moved in, the place fell vacant again, allegedly due to 'certain problems'. It is unclear what these 'problems' might have been, but it was said that the fairies had taken exception to the occupancy and had disturbed the man with unearthly cries and shrieks. He quickly moved out. Once again, the Clearys applied for tenancy of the cottage, and this time they were successful. It is suspected that their move created some local resentment—after all, compared to many of their neighbours, the couple were regarded as reasonably well-off, and Bridget was thought to have 'airs' about her. The new cottage reflected their supposedly 'grand' status about their neighbours

Making ends meet

Despite Bridget's airs, the family soon fell into rent arrears—not uncommon in the district but puzzling given the Clearys' relatively prosperous status. They were so badly in arrears that the Poor Law Guardians forbade any repair work to be carried out until the debt was cleared.
At Tullowcossaun, they were surrounded by relatives. Mary Kennedy, Bridget's aunt, lived a short distance away at Ballyvadlea Bridge. Mary's sons Patrick, James, and William lived with her. Mary's daughter, Johanna (known as 'Han' or 'Hannie'), lived nearby with her. husband Michael Burke and their children. Bridget had been Johanna's bridesmaid and the two were reasonably close.
From the time she came to live at Tullowcossaun, Bridget continued to show a strong and independent spirit. Michael was still working in Clonmel, and it was up to her to run the house and provide for her widowed father. She still did some dressmaking, although not as much as before, but she now had another source of income—she kept hens. They were an important source of income, and they gave Bridget some financial independence. She sold eggs 'on tick', collecting the money for her produce around the start of each month. There were some problems with this arrangement, however, as not everybody was willing or able to pay when she called; some of her neighbours ran up large bills.
The winter of 1894/95 was severe. Snow, ice, and hard frosts delayed farm work long after Christmas, and many labourers

found themselves without wages. It was not until late March that the weather picked up and working conditions improved. For the Clearys, the situation was not so desperate because Michael was not dependent on seasonal work. For Bridget, however, it meant payment from eggs already sold would be hard to come by.

The Trouble Begins

On 4 March 1895, Bridget walked from her home across Ballyvadlea Bridge towards Kylenagranagh Hill. It was here. that 'fairy man' Jack Dunne lived with his wife Kate, and Bridget was calling to collect outstanding money for eggs. Dunne's dwelling was empty.

Jack and Kate Dunne had no children and spent much of their time in the local pubs. Bridget waited for a while, feeling the cold penetrating her clothes—for winter still had a firm grip on the land—and then walked home, entering her own house shivering. She tried to warm herself at the fire, but, according to her cousin Johanna, it was no use. She had caught what the country people called a 'founder', a severe and penetrating chill.

The shivering fit hadn't passed by the next day, and Bridget now complained of a severe headache. Great attention was paid to the place where she had received the 'founder' and her reasons for being there. Living near the sinister Kylenagranagh Hill, Jack Dunne was said to be 'well in' with the fairies and was widely regarded as a seanachai and a custodian of ancient lore.

Jack claimed to have seen fairies on numerous occasions playing hurling near his door in the evening light. He frequently complained of back pain, which he said occurred. one night when the fairies lifted him out of his bed and threw him into the yard. He claimed to know the fairies intimately and had even been up Kylenagranagh Hill with them.
Such talk often secured drinks for Jack and his wife. He was treated with a great deal of respect—to demand money from a man so friendly with the fairies might invite disaster. Maybe that was what Bridget Cleary's 'founder' was all about.

Bridget the Changeling
Bridget went to bed, but her condition grew worse. She may have caught pneumonia, but she remained untreated. Doctors were few and far between—and very expensive. Far better to fetch the 'fairy doctor.' And so it was that Jack Dunne made his way to Tullowcossaun.

Although able to sit at the fire, take some food, and walk around a little, Bridget was certainly not her former self. Dunne sat with her for a while. Squinting in the smoky light, the old man looked at the young woman. His words were to have a dramatic effect on subsequent events.
'That is not Bridget Boland,' he whispered. In other circumstances, this remark might have been taken differently, but coming from the lips of a 'fairy man' it had a particular resonance. Jack was articulating what some were thinking anyway—the real Bridget had been spirited away. and

replaced by a stock' or 'pattern' of herself. This was no longer a woman but a'sheehoguey' that had come down from Kylenagranagh Hill to take her place.

Bridget had several enemies amongst her neighbours—the envious, the suitors she had snubbed, and those who considered her too 'high and mighty.' Some remarked on how this proud, independent woman had suddenly turned into an invalid. The reason for such sudden and rapid deterioration had to be a supernatural one. There was one other indication that this might be the case: although married for over seven years, Michael and Bridget were childless, a sure hint of fairy involvement.

Dunne was asked to look at the invalid more closely. Upon doing so, he suggested that she was indeed a fairy. One leg, he stated, was longer than the other, a sure sign that she was 'fairy-struck'. While he was measuring Bridget, Michael Cleary arrived at the house to find him there. He paid close attention to everything Jack Dunne had to say, taking the old man's opinions to heart.

'This is not my wife at all. This is not Bridget,' Michael muttered to himself. 'It's a fairy creature from Kylenagranagh Hill.' But although he was suspicious, he did nothing about it.

Bridget's illness grows worse.

Bridget's condition worsened over the next few days. By Saturday, March, she was barely able to stir herself from her bed. Her cousin Johanna Burke believed that she'd caught a fresh chill or that the 'founder' had got a real hold on her.

Despite the 'consultation' with Jack Dunne, it was considered that a trained medical doctor should be sent. Patrick Boland walked the four miles to Fethard to ask Dr. William Crean to call the house and look at his daughter. On his journey to the doctor's surgery, he stopped at the house of one of the poor law guardians to get the red ticket, which entitled Bridget to a medical examination under the Poor Law scheme. He then walked to the dispensary in Fethard and asked Crean to visit the house.

The weekend passed, and the doctor still had not come. The weather was changing—gales were blowing and the days were dull and wet; the road into Ballyvadlea was muddy and covered with blown-down branches and leaves. Perhaps Crean didn't fancy travelling into that remote area on what he might have considered to be a 'charity case';
Perhaps he was busy elsewhere. There were also stories that the good doctor was a bit too fond of the bottle for his own good and that he haphazardly attended to his medical duties.

From late Sunday and all through Monday, it rained very heavily, nearly flooding the roads, but as the evening wore on, it began to ease. There was still no sign of Dr. Crean, but, all the while, Bridget's condition appeared to grow steadily worse. Johanna Burke was convinced that she now had a fever and that a doctor must be brought as a matter of urgency. On Monday afternoon, Michael Cleary himself walked to Fethard to remind the doctor, but still Crean didn't come. Nor did he come on Tuesday.

On Wednesday, 13 March, Michael Cleary again walked the four miles to Fethard to see if the doctor would come, and he also sent a message to Drangan Chapel to ask Father Cornelius Ryan if he would come to attend to his wife, who was dying. This did the trick, and on Wednesday afternoon, Dr Crean finally called the Cleary home. His examination may have been cursory, and the diagnosis was swift and perfunctory. Bridget was suffering from 'nervous excitement' coupled with a slight bronchitis. He prescribed medicine and went back to Fethard.

Later, at Michael Cleary's trial, he would reveal that he didn't know if the family had obtained the medicine, nor could he give any cause for the 'excitement'. But he would reveal that Bridget had been attending his surgery in Fethard for 'about six to eight months', although he didn't say why. The popular belief was that she had a tubercular condition and that she had been attending the TB clinic in Clonmel.

Bridget's illness was now beginning to have an impact on the immediate family. Michael Cleary was sinking deeper and deeper into depression, and Patrick Boland was becoming increasingly worried about his daughter's condition. He asked his sister, Mary Kennedy, to call on her, and she said that she would bring Johanna Burke, who lived nearby at Rathkenny. When Han Burke arrived, both she and Bridget got into an earnest conversation, and Johanna thought that there was some sort of marital difficulty between Bridget and her husband, but this remained unspecified. 'He's making a fairy of me,' complained the invalid. In local parlance, this meant that Michael Cleary was distancing himself from her for some reason. Johanna Burke also knew that Michael Cleary had had frequent disagreements with his mother-in-law and that he thought that the 'fairy woman' had passed on some of her rumoured arcane powers and skills to her daughter, making the brooding and superstitious man nervous of his wife. Even with these visitors and the almost forced merriment going on in the house, Bridget's condition didn't improve. If she was taking Doctor Crean's medicine, it had no apparent effect on her. As he looked from his doorway to distant Slievenamon, Michael Cleary wondered what he should do about his wife. He had tried to bring Doctor Crean to the house no less than three times, and when he finally did come, his diagnosis had been unsatisfactory.

The Fairy Man
There was another option, of course: Jack Dunne had suggested that the family consult with Denis Ganey, a 'fairy man' over in Kylatlea on the lower slopes of the mountain. And so, on Thursday, 14 March, Michael Cleary set out for Slievenamon.

According to contemporary accounts, Denis Ganey was a middle-aged man, rather tall and with a heavy beard. Like Jack Dunne and several other 'fairy men', he walked with a limp, having one leg shorter than the other.

According to Michael Cleary, Ganey listened very attentively, asking several questions about Bridget's condition, and then handed over something like, 'According to contemporary accounts,

Denis Ganey was a middle-aged man, rather tall and with a heavy beard. Like Jack Dunne and several other 'fairy men', he walked with a limp, having The meeting with Ganey had a powerful effect on Cleary, and he returned home in a highly agitated state. It is reasonable to suppose that the 'cure' that he'd obtained from 'Ganey over the mountain' probably contained more (foxglove), which was supposed to 'burn the entrails out of any fairy or unearthly creature'. It had to be mixed with the 'bee stings', the first milk drawn from a cow directly after calving into a bucket in which a silver coin had been placed.

If the charm did contain a substantial amount of foxglove, then it was poisonous and would only have worsened Bridget's condition. But Michael Cleary, who believed in charms and 'fairy potions', was determined that she should have it. After the meeting with Denis Ganey, he was now more convinced than ever that Bridget was a changeling and that, if not dealt with, she would work a malign influence on him and his family. Perhaps it was Ganey who had put the notion in his head, but he was now convinced that the real Bridget Cleary had been abducted by the fairy king and was now being held prisoner somewhere beneath Kylenagranagh Hill, having been replaced by some awful supernatural thing that had to be driven out.

That same evening, a crowd of neighbours, including the Burkes and the Simpsons, called at the Cleary house to see how Bridget was. As they approached the building, they heard a man's voice from inside. shout angrily: 'Take that, you bitch!' Pausing outside the place, a couple of them tried to look in through the window, but the shutters were drawn and they could see nothing. They knocked on the door, but from inside, Michael Cleary's voice told them that they couldn't come in yet.

A Brutal Scene
For some minutes, the neighbours waited outside the door while voices inside the house screamed and shouted. They heard snatches of a heated conversation: 'Take it, you old bitch!' or 'Take it, you witch!' Then, to everyone's surprise, the door suddenly flew open, and from somewhere inside, a man's voice cried, 'Away she goes!" Michael Cleary came to the doorway, apparently bathed in sweat, and invited his neighbours in. They looked at him strangely, and he explained that he had kept the door closed because the house had been full of fairies.

One of the first through the door was Johanna Burke, and, she was to say later, the scene that greeted them was one of brutal horror. Patrick Boland was sitting in the kitchen by the light of a large oil lamp, but everyone else was in the bedroom. Bridget Cleary was lying on the bed with Jack Dunne (who was not a sturdy man), forcibly holding her head down by the ears. Her cousin Patrick Kennedy was on the far side of the bed, gripping her right arm, while his brother James held her left. The younger brother, William, lay across her legs to prevent her from moving them and from trying to get up. They were forcing her to take something on a spoon from a small black saucepan, which Jack Dunne called 'a pint'.

Later, a report in the Irish Times, covering Michael Cleary's trial, stated: 'Cleary was giving her medicine—some herbs on a spoon. Bridget Cleary was trying not to take it. She said that it was too bitter. When Cleary put the milk into the mouth, he put his hand on her mouth to prevent the medicine from coming up. He said that if it went on the ground, she could not be brought back from the fairies. Cleary asked her if she was Bridget Cleary or Bridget Boland, wife of Michael Cleary, in the Name of God. He asked her more than once. She answered three times before he was satisfied.'

It seems that Michael Cleary succeeded in forcing at least some of the herbal mixture down his wife's throat. He managed about three doses of the stuff while his neighbours were there and is said to have made her swallow a further three before they arrived. When this was done, all the men who were present shouted, 'Away with you! Come home, Bridget Boland, in the Name of God!' Then they clapped their hands and slapped her.

However, one of the neighbours who had just come in paid close attention to great burn marks across the invalid's forehead, and it was later discovered that she had been threatened with a red-hot poker to make her take the herbs. Hearing the voices of the visitors in the kitchen, Bridget screamed. Then Michael Cleary asked his wife again, 'Are you Bridget Boland, wife of Michael Cleary, in the Name of God?' Bridget seemed to make no answer, or else her reply was so weak and faint that nobody in the room could hear it. Turning to her husband, Jack Dunne said, 'Make a good fire and we will make her answer.'

The fire had already been burning quite well in the open hearth, even though no fuel had been added to it. Gathering around her, the men lifted Bridget bodily from the bed, 'winding' her in the bedclothes, and carried her to the grave. Jack Dunne took her head and James Kennedy her feet, Michael Cleary following with the spoon and saucepan. According to Johanna Burke, Bridget seemed fully conscious and well aware of what was going on.

With little effort, the men held her over the steadily burning flames. With desperation edging his voice, Patrick Boland asked, 'Are you the daughter of Patrick Boland, the wife of Michael Cleary?' Bridget, clearly terrified, struggled a little. 'I am, Dada,' she answered clearly. The men continued to hold her over the flames for at least ten minutes before carrying her back to bed. After subjecting her to this 'ordeal by fire,' it may have been that they felt temporarily convinced that they had driven the witchlike creature out.

The Priest Calls

At about 7.00 am on Friday, 15 March, Father Cornelius Ryan was called from the parochial house at Drangan to visit Bridget. The priest had called on her two days before, as requested, and was told that she was dying. He had given her the last rites of the church, but he refused to come when called upon that Thursday. Now Michael Cleary turned up at his door once more and asked him to come. Somewhat reluctantly, Father Ryan did so.

He arrived at the house sometime after 8.00 am, said Mass in Bridget's bedroom, and gave her Holy Communion. Bridget, however, was reputed not to have swallowed the sacred host (according to the testimony given later by her cousin Johanna) but to have surreptitiously removed it from her mouth with her fingers—something expressly forbidden by Catholic teaching. If this indeed happened, the action may have sealed her fate because it was well known that neither she nor the fairy could bear the touch of the Blessed Host on their tongue.

As well as that, both witches and evildoers often used the Wafer in the preparation of pishogues (charms or spells) and dark magics.

Whether this was communicated to Michael Cleary isn't known, but if it was, it would have undoubtedly strengthened his belief about his wife. Father Ryan asked him if he was still giving her the medicine that Doctor Crean had prescribed, but Cleary said that he had no faith in it. The priest seemed to concur as he spoke of William Crean as being 'always drunk'.

During the afternoon, an argument of some kind appears to have developed between Johanna Burke and Michael Cleary about payment for the milk that the former alleged she had sold to Bridget. According to the evidence given later by Johanna Burke, 'Mrs. Cleary asked her husband if I was paid for the milk. I said yes and showed her the shilling, which she took and put under the blankets and gave it back again in a minute.'

This incident later seems to have been the source of some trouble between husband and wife, for Michael Cleary withheld milk from Bridget when she asked for it later in the day. It seems that he later accused his wife of having rubbed the shilling on her leg when she put it under the blankets and interpreted this as a sinister action on her part as if she were making a spell or 'pishogue'. The incident also highlights Johanna Burke's possibly ambivalent attitude towards her cousin, of whom she may have disapproved or been jealous.

That evening, some neighbours called to see how Bridget was progressing. In tightly knit country communities, this was to be taken as 'good neighbourliness', but they may have been motivated to come by curiosity as well. They sat in the kitchen, and later Johanna Burke joined them, making them stir fry (porridge).

Because there were visitors, Cleary got his wife out of bed, had her dressed, and brought her in amongst the company. One of the visitors, Tom Smith, asked how she was keeping, and she replied that she was middling' but that her husband was making a fairy of her'. She referred to the fact that her husband would not allow her to drink any of the milk that Johanna had bought and that she had never asked for milk without buying it.

Later that night, Johanna Burke's brothers (Bridget's cousins) Patrick, James, and William arrived back from Michael. Cleary's father's wake, which had been held in Killenaule eight miles away. (Michael Cleary's father had died the day before, but his son had not attended the wake). owing, apparently, to his wife's illness). Towards midnight some of the neighbours left so that now only the immediate members of the family were left—Bridget and her husband, her father Patrick Boland, her aunt Mary Kennedy, her cousins, and her cousin Johanna's young daughter Katie.

A Horror

As Bridget was being handed a cup of tea, Michael Cleary got three pieces of bread and jam and insisted that she eat them before she drank the tea. He suddenly asked, 'Are you Bridget Cleary, my wife, in the Name of God?' He asked this three times, and she answered him twice, and he ate two of the pieces of bread and jam. When she didn't answer a third time, he rose from where he'd been sitting and forced the third piece of bread to jam down her throat, shouting, 'Swallow it! Is it down? Is it down?' He then struck her across the face, flinging her from her seat and onto the earthen floor of the cottage.

Desperately, Bridget called on her cousin to intervene—' Oh, Han! Han!'—but!' Mrs. Burke did nothing. Perhaps she was frightened of the violent Michael Cleary, who now, in a fit of even greater rage, tore off most of his wife's clothing, leaving her in her chemise in front of the men. Taking a burning stick from the grate, he brandished it in front of her face, as if trying to ram it down her throat. Then, taking the house key, he crossed to the door and turned it in the lock, effectively locking everyone in the cottage.

At this point, terrified by his demented behaviour, Mrs. Burke withdrew into the bedroom. Her role in the events and failure to come to her cousin's aid when she was in mortal danger seem unclear; perhaps she felt unable to intervene between husband and wife because local propriety forbade that. A few of the others who remained—Johanna's mother, Mrs Kennedy, for instance—had also earlier gone into the bedroom for a bit of a doze.
Johanna heard Bridget shout, 'Give me a chance!', then she heard her head strike the floor and heard her scream. The kitchen must have been a scene of chaos. Michael Cleary was now apparently standing over his wife with the still-burning stick, jerking it at her and threatening her. He jerked it close to her body, and it took only a minute for the calico chemise to catch fire.
In the bedroom beyond, Mary Kennedy was hardly more than dozing when she heard her son William cry out from the kitchen: 'Mother! Mother! Bridgie is burned!' She rose, and

both she and Johanna Burke shouted, 'What ails you?' Michael Cleary met them at the bedroom door and, with a solemn face, turned to Mrs Burke and said, 'I believe she's dead!' Then, walking over to the window, he took down a lamp and, unscrewing a cap, poured paraffin all over the prone body on the floor.

There is no doubt that he was now out of control, and as he attempted to set fire to Bridget, he was stopped by Mrs. Kennedy, whom he pushed away. 'What are you doing with the creature?' cried the old woman as she reeled back. 'Is it roasting her you are?' Michael Cleary suddenly darted forward and set fire to his wife's paraffin-soaked body, which was ablaze in an instant. The recklessness of this act was underlined by the fact that he could easily have set the whole house on fire and all of its occupants.

'For the love of God, Michael!' James Kennedy, who had risen from Patrick Boland's bed where he'd been sleeping, had come to the bedroom door and had witnessed the horror. 'Don't burn your wife!' Half-turning, Cleary looked at him blankly. 'She's not my wife', he answered in a low, flat voice. 'She's an old deceiver sent in place of my wife. She's been deceiving me for the last seven or eight days and deceived the priest today too, but she won't deceive me anymore. As I begin with her, I will finish it with her. You'll soon see her go up the chimney!' By this, he referred to the traditional escape route for a changeling.

Seeing that the man's wits were gone, William Kennedy, who had come down to the Cleary house with his mother, asked him for the house key so that they might go, but Cleary only drew a knife and told him that the door wouldn't be opened again until the real Bridget had been returned to him from her imprisonment under Kylenagranagh Hill. Waving the weapon at William, he threatened to 'run him through' if he attempted to leave. The boy fainted clean away.

Turning to the rest of the family, Cleary warned them, 'If you come out any more, I'll roast you as well as her.' Everyone withdrew into the bedroom, leaving Cleary alone with his burning wife. Still holding the lamp, he threw oil on her three times before sitting down on a chair to watch the flames rise. Some of the others peeped out of the bedroom, and Cleary turned towards them shouting, 'You're a dirty set! You'd rather have her with the fairies in Kylenagranagh than have her here with me!'

Patrick Boland came out of the room and informed Cleary that if there was anything that he could do to save his daughter, then he would do it. Cleary told him that he could bury her with her mother, who had also been 'of the fairy'. He further told him that next Sunday, he (Cleary) would go to Kylengranagh Fort, where the real Bridget would come riding to him on a white horse, and that if he could cut the golden straps that bound her to the animal, she would be free and would be his once more. This was what 'Ganey over the mountain' had told him, although he would later declare that Bridget had told him it herself. As he spoke, Johanna Burke later told the court, the house was filled with smoke, and flames crackled around Bridget's body.

Later, under duress, Patrick Kennedy went with Michael Cleary to bury the body at a secret spot nearby, the rest of the family remaining locked in the house by Cleary. Once the body had been buried, Cleary made all who had witnessed the atrocity kneel and swear on the Holy Name not to reveal it to a soul. He would subsequently tell those who asked that Bridget had simply 'gone away'.

The Fallout
The next day, Saturday, March 16, Jack Dunne, badly agitated, accompanied Michael Cleary and Michael Kennedy to Drangan village to attend confession in the chapel there. Although Father Ryan was the parish priest—and he seems to have been largely sympathetic towards Michael Cleary, on the surface at least—it was the curate, Father McGrath, who took confession that day.
John Dunne went into the box first and spoke quietly to the curate, who told him to send Michael Cleary (who was in the chapel yard) in to see him. Cleary came in and, weeping, spoke to Father McGrath, although what was said remains under the seal of the Confessional. The curate, however, deemed that he was 'in no fit state to receive absolution'. He went to fetch Father Ryan and the three of them talked for a long time.
All the while, Michael Kennedy remained outside in the chapel yard. Eventually, Father Ryan emerged and walked straight across the road and into the Drangan police barracks.

Again, nobody knows what was said by the parish priest to Acting Sergeant Patrick Egan inside the barracks, but it was enough to arouse police suspicions. Egan was well known in the locality, and he had already probably heard the weird stories that were circulating about Michael Cleary and the mysterious disappearance of his wife. However, he couldn't investigate without a formal complaint being lodged, especially in a tightly-knit rural community like Ballyvadlea. Taking another policeman with him, Egan followed Michael Cleary along the Fethard road, and, as he stopped at Mary Kennedy's cottage, the policeman approached him and asked him about his wife. Sticking to his original story, Cleary informed him that she had left home 'about twelve o'clock last night' although he hadn't seen her going as he had been in bed at the time, asleep (adding that he hadn't slept for about eight nights previously). Egan walked home with him, repeating his questions from time to time.

Cleary always answered that Bridget was gone, but he didn't know where. As he left the house, Egan heard Patrick Boland shout from inside, 'My daughter will come back to me!' The old man would insist right up to his trial that his daughter was alive and well and was living 'elsewhere' (with the fairies). Despite Michael Cleary's assurances, Egan was suspicious and asked for more police from Clonmel to be drafted into Ballyvadlea. Their mission was to look for Bridget.

A lover's revenge?

Shortly after these men arrived, there was a formal complaint made against Michael Cleary. The name of the complainant has never been disclosed, but it is thought to have been William Simpson, long reputed to be Bridget Cleary's lover. Simpson was to claim that Michael Cleary had approached him for the loan of a revolver (which Simpson was known to keep about him) so that he could go up to Kylenagranagh Fort and 'bring back his wife'.

Simpson didn't lend him the gun, but he later claimed to have seen him going up the hill carrying a large table knife. Allegedly, Cleary had waited there a long time for Bridget to appear on a white horse, but he had seen nothing. By now, the situation had become too serious and too complex for the Drangan police station to handle, and Patrick Egan passed the case to Inspector Joseph Wansborough in Carrick-on-Suir, who ordered a full-scale search of the area around the Clearys' cottage.

Police were soon searching the areas of Drangan, Clooneen, and Mullinahone. Wansborough visited several homes around Ballyvadlea and took copious notes from those whom he interviewed. He soon obtained his first formal, sworn statement. It came from William Simpson and was given on Monday, March 18, before W. Walker Tennant, Justice of the Peace.

Simpson stated that he had witnessed Bridget Cleary being ill-treated in her home on the previous Thursday night. He also named at least some of the people whom he knew to

have been there and whom he considered responsible. Once again, police swarmed through the area. and those whom Simpson had named were questioned. Johanna Burke went separately to Justice Walker Tennant and swore some further 'information' in front of him, to the effect that Bridget Cleary had left her home while sick and had 'disappeared'.
The Justice then asked Wansborough if charges would be brought against anyone. Strangely, given that he now had so much concrete information regarding the case, the first person that Wansborough charged was the defendant, Denis Ganey. He was charged with 'causing Bridget Cleary to be ill-treated and great actual bodily harm done to her'. This was bizarre since it is supposed that Ganey had never even met Bridget Cleary, even if his influence on events had been profound. All the same, the police net was beginning to tighten around Michael Cleary.

On Friday, 22 March 1895, officers from the Royal Irish Constabulary, guided by William Simpson, searched an area of boggy ground in the area of Tullowcossaun, near the Cleary home. Away in the corner of a field, about a quarter-mile from the cottage, Sergeant Patrick Rogers of the Mullinahone Constabulary noticed some freshly turned earth and crushed bushes. Constables Somers and O'Callaghan helped him dig down about eighteen inches, where they found a dirty sheet wrapped around what seemed to be a woman's body.

The corpse itself had been pulled up into a crouching position with the knees almost up against the chin, and the body was very badly burnt. It was naked except for a few remnants of clothing, all badly charred, which had been seared into the skin, and a pair of black stockings. The head was covered in a sack and was largely untouched. There was still a gold earring in one of the ears. Tearing away the coarse sacking, Rogers looked at the face and identified it. They had found what remained of Bridget Cleary.

Nine people arrested
Now that her body had been found, arrests followed swiftly. Police took several people from Ballyvadlea and Tullowcossaun. districts, including Michael Cleary, Patrick Boland, Bridget's father, Mary Kennedy, Johanna Burke, the Kennedy brothers, and Jack Dunne.
All across Ireland and far beyond, interest was suddenly focused on a remote area of County Tipperary as the incident became widely known as 'The Clonmel Witch Burning'. Soon obscure Ballyvadlea was known halfway around the world as a place of dark superstition and sinister events. Indeed, elements of the British and Unionist press tried to make political capital of the affair by proclaiming it as evidence of the backwardness of the Irish peasantry and their unfitness for

Home Rule.

The defendants were arraigned at the Summer Assizes in Clonmel and were brought to trial on 4 July 1895. The judge, Mr Justice O'Brien, paid scant attention to the talk of fairies and 'witchcraft' and showed little sympathy for Cleary's state of mind at the time. All the same, the talk persisted and was readily seized on by the press. All this rumour did not affect Michael Cleary's ultimate sentence—he received twenty years' penal servitude for the manslaughter of his wife. Jack Dunne and the Kennedy brothers (who had assisted in forcing Ganey's poison down Bridget's throat) were found guilty of 'wounding.' Patrick Kennedy was sentenced to five years imprisonment, Jack Dunne to three, and the other two were sentenced to one year each. Patrick Boland and Michael Kennedy each received a sentence of six months, but Mary Kennedy was set free by order of the court.

There was some speculation that Mary Kennedy had given information that had helped convict the others, but this is far from certain. Early on, her daughter Johanna Burke revoked the first statement she had made to the police and turned Queen's evidence: in the trial, she became the chief witness for the prosecution, and the evidence she provided was crucial.

From the Assizes at Clonmel, the prisoners were taken to Mountjoy Prison. Jack Dunne was later released on licence and returned to Ballyvadlea. His wife Kate had died, and he is said to have finished his days as a labouring man, broken and unwilling to talk about the incident.

The Kennedys too were released on licence and returned home to work as labourers, refusing to say anything. Michael Cleary, however, remained in prison, being shunted between Mountjoy in Dublin and Maryborough (now Portlaoise) Prison in County Laois.

According to some accounts, Cleary learned to work as a tailor and was a rather quiet and withdrawn inmate. He was released on licence from Maryborough on 28 April 1910. It is unclear whether he returned briefly to County Tipperary; some argue that he never returned as 'he couldn't show his face in the countryside'. What is known is that in June of that same year, he boarded a ship bound, via Liverpool, to Montreal and vanished from the pages of recorded history. It is possible that when he arrived in Canada, he changed his name and disappeared.

Heading

The horrors of the 'Clonmel witch burning' still lie somewhere deep in the memories of the people who live in Ballyvadlea today, and there are few in the countryside who are willing to talk about it. The area remains very close-knit, and there are descendants of all the main participants in the case living there still. The community, understandably, wishes to consign the whole affair to history.

Some vestiges of the Cleary house remain, although the original house itself has long been converted into another dwelling and, as such, is not accessible to the public. Kylenagranagh Hill is still there, of course, but much of the fort, which once dominated its crown, has been cleared away. It still has a sinister reputation, and some old people of the area will tell you privately that the fairies still hold court there on certain nights of the year.

Despite the passage of time, the reticence of local people, and the changes to the countryside, the case still holds a fascination for the general public, perhaps because it happened comparatively recently (just over a century ago) and sporadic tours of the 'Tipperary, which country' continue to be well subscribed, especially by visitors from overseas. Bridget Cleary seems ultimately to have been the victim of the eerie superstition that ebbed and flowed through the pleasant Tipperary countryside like a black tide. The local schoolchildren still sing an odd and slightly sinister rhyme as they play their skipping games:
 'Are you a witch, or are you a fairy? Are you the wife of Michael Cleary?'

 It is not clear if Cleary ever returned to his home; he returned briefly to County Tipperary; some argue that he never returned as 'he couldn't show his face in the countryside'. What is known is that in June of that same year, he boarded a ship bound, via Liverpool, to Montreal and vanished from the pages of recorded history. It is possible that when he arrived in Canada, he changed his name and disappeared.

Heading

The horrors of the 'Clonmel witch burning' still lie somewhere deep in the memories of the people who live in Ballyvadlea today, and there are few in the countryside who are willing to talk about it. The area remains very close-knit and there are descendants of all the main participants in the case living there still.

The community, understandably, wishes to consign the whole affair to history.

Some vestiges of the Cleary house remain, although the original house itself has long been converted into another dwelling and, as such, is not accessible to the public. Kylenagranagh Hill is still there, of course, but much of the fort, which once dominated its crown, has been cleared away. It still has a sinister reputation, and some old people of the area will tell you privately that the fairies still hold court there on certain nights of the year.

Despite the passage of time, the reticence of local people, and the changes to the countryside, the case still holds a fascination for the general public, perhaps because it happened comparatively recently (just over a century ago) and sporadic tours of the 'Tipperary, which country' continue to be well subscribed, especially by visitors from overseas. Bridget Cleary seems ultimately to have been the victim of the eerie superstition that ebbed and flowed through the pleasant Tipperary countryside like a black tide. The local schoolchildren still sing an odd and slightly sinister rhyme as they play their skipping games.

'Are you a witch, or are you a fairy? Are you the wife of Michael Cleary?'

The Changeling.

Bridget Cleary was certainly a slightly unusual woman by the standards of the time, but there are no facts to point to anything untoward. Although witches, changelings, and assorted superstitions were common cultural beliefs at the time, and as a child, she went regularly to the Faery Fort nearby. It was here that she would whisper her dreams and secrets to the Faery folk.

a family of three brothers and both of her parents.

As a child, she was a bit of a dreamer, the only daughter of Patrick and Bridget Bowland.

Born in 1867 near Clonmel, in the south of County Tipperary, she was the only daughter and youngest child of Patrick and Bridget Boland. They were both staunch Catholics, and she was raised in the same vein, attending a convent school, as was quite normal for the time. She demonstrated an aptitude for needlework and became apprenticed to a dressmaker. She went on to marry Michael Cleary, a cooper, who was nine years older than her.

They lived apart for nine months, with Bridget moving home to look after her ailing mother while Michael continued in his old job.

It was only after her mother died that Michael joined Bridget and Patrick and her father in their small cottage.

The villagers had always considered that Bridget was not only charmed in her life but also much loved by the faeries.

When a brand new cottage was built of stone, the couple applied for it. Their first attempt failed, and it went to another couple, but when the couple experienced strange noises and discovered their home was built on a faery road, they promptly moved out.

This time Bridget and Michael were successful and moved into the cottage with Bridget's father.

The only daughter with three older brothers, she grew up being the apple of her family's eye. Perhaps this caused her to feel a little superior to everyone else, as many of the villagers described her as being aloof and prideful.

Certainly, she doesn't seem to have had many friends, and being sent away to learn dressmaking could only have made things worse.

This was a career that meant she could dress herself in fashionable clothes and earn a decent income. A thing practically unheard of in the society she lived in.

Many people seemed to take Bridget's independence as an affront to the dictates of society at that time. Bridget refused to conform. She did love and respect her husband, but she would be damned if she would live in penury for the sake of his pride. As for the neighbours, well, they could mind their own business. Many people seemed to take Bridget's independence as an affront to the dictates of society at that time. Bridget refused to conform. She did love and respect her husband, but she would be damned if she would live in penury for the sake of his pride. As for the neighbours, well, they could mind their own business.

Many people seemed to take Bridget's independence as an affront to the dictates of society at that time. Bridget refused to conform. She did love and respect her husband, but she would be damned if she would live in penury for the sake of his pride. As for the neighbours, well, they could mind their own business.

Passing by the fairy mound, she left a fine brown egg as an offering and walked on. She enjoyed seeing the snowdrops, which were a bit late this year; new buds were appearing on the trees, and despite the wind and the leftover snow, the signs of spring were everywhere.

On reaching Jack Dunne's house, she was surprised to find him out, finding this strange as Dunne himself had specifically asked that she drop them off. Her irritation with her cousin grew; recently he had been stuck to her husband like a limpet; every time she turned around, he seemed to be there watching her and whispering in Michael's ear.

Irritated, she turned back for home, deciding that Dunne could pick up his eggs if he wanted them.

Approaching the fairy raffle, she decided to go and speak with the fairy.

He had quite a bit on her mind, not least the gap that seemed to be getting wider by the day between her and Michael. And Jack Dunne seemed to be making things worse.

She lay down on the mound and started to cry, then she told the faeries her worries.

She spoke of Michael's pride that he would sooner live in poverty than allow Bridget to work and that she had no intention of stopping.

"Did the faery hear her? Did they care even if they did?" We will never know. By the time she got home, she had a very bad headache, and she couldn't get warm even sitting by the fire. Michael was in a foul mood that day. Still struggling to find work as well as jealous and confused by his wife's success, it is believed that Michael and Bridget fought that morning over baseless accusations of adultery.

Michael had a lot of time on his hands, and most of it was spent tormenting himself over what his wife was up to when she was out of the house. He worried about the fairies and became enraged and embarrassed that Bridget was effectively the family's provider. Even if Bridget suggested Michael join her on the delivery route, he would have refused.

To Michael Cleary, the only thing worse than staying home while your wife worked was working with her in a business she created. Michael believed Bridget was changing. He may not have been completely wrong. Reports from some who knew the couple claimed he criticised her hours away from home, methods of prayer, and choice in clothing—even taking issue with the undergarments she chose to wear. Michael's idea of a proper wife was set in stone, and there was no room for a woman looking to change and progress. As difficult as their home life was becoming, there is no evidence to suggest that Bridget was interested in anything other than finding balance with her troubled husband.

She was an evolving independent woman, yes, but she still held tight to her Catholic faith and believed in the sanctity of her marriage. Bridget decided not to back down and bend to Michael's will. As far as she was concerned, he was more than welcome at her side. If he would prefer to sulk at home all day, that was his choice. In the days leading up to her murder.

Bridget had fallen ill. She was suffering from a sore throat and terrible coughing fits that were made worse by long treks through cold wetlands. She became disoriented while wandering through the moors and was said to have been lost for several hours before stumbling home. Her father and Michael were present when she finally arrived. Her father was concerned and urged her to get to bed, but Michael was completely horrified at her condition. The sick woman was confused, fevered, and clearly in need of medical attention. The stuttering, sickly woman struggling to stand up on her own did not resemble the Bridget Cleary Michael knew.

This only strengthened Michael's resolve to stop Bridget from wandering around on her own. This was the excuse that he had been waiting for. To most, these would be clear signs of a severe illness. To the frustrated and suppressed Mr Cleary, the symptoms were signifiers of something else. If Michael had been harbouring any deep desire to harm Bridget, this had given him the perfect excuse. By the following day, she was much worse; her father feared for her life and walked four miles in the wind and rain to request a visit from the doctor.

Being told that the doctor couldn't visit for at least three days, Patrick had a four-mile trek home, despair in his heart.

Mary Kennedy steps outside her front door. The wind whips her face and almost knocks her over. Still, family is family, and she had promised her brother Patrick that she would call in and visit her niece.

On the way, she meets Jack Dunne, and together they walk on to Bridget's house.

Mary was shocked by Bridget's appearance; the young woman in this bed had no resemblance to the beautiful and smartly dressed young woman she knew and, saying so, noticed how quickly Jack Dunne jumped at what was a throwaway comment and declared in a loud voice, "I have told the man (meaning Michael) that that creature upstairs is not our Bridget." The seeds were now sown.

7th March

Michael goes to fetch the doctor, declaring that he will be bringing him back, even if he has to carry him over his shoulder.

Michael was true to his word and brought the doctor back, even though he was slightly inebriated. In the house at that time were our old friend Jack Dunne, Mary Kennedy, and Mary's daughter, Joanna Burke. Mary's daughter and Bridget's cousin. After examining Bridget, he diagnoses nervous stress and mild bronchitis. He leaves a bottle of medicine. With the medicine not seeming to make much difference, Dunne persuades Michael to visit the local Faery. Dr Patrick now desperately complies and walks six miles to the home of Denis Ganey, who, after brewing given the facts that suited Jack Dunne, concurred and pronounced that this is faery possession. Giving Michael the directions that the herbs must be boiled in new milk (new milk is a cow's first lactation after birthing a calf). This bolstered Dunne's confidence, and now he spoke openly that the real Bridget was gone and the creature upstairs was an old hag, a changeling.

9Th March

Father Cornelious Rhyan is summoned to give the last rites. Bridget's bedroom is packed with family and neighbours. There are conflicting reports as to whether or not Michael initially sent for a medical doctor in the first place or simply told his father-in-law he had At this period in Ireland, most villages had few, if any, doctors. If someone fell ill, a doctor had to be sent. The journey could take precious days, which it did in Bridget's case. Some neighbours believed Michael had sent for Jack instead, only relenting to call for a real doctor at the anger and insistence of Patrick. In either case, Jack Dunne arrived and examined Bridget. His diagnosis confirmed Michael's superstitious fears.

The woman in his home was not even a real woman; it was an evil fairy changeling. Jack and Michael got to work planning folk cures to dispel the changeling. If Patrick was sceptical at first, the urging of both his nephew and son-in-law eventually swayed him. Within a day, he had decided to help the other men with their nonsensical mission. Patrick would claim he truly had begun to believe Bridget was in danger. The medical doctor arrived days later and diagnosed Bridget with a severe case of bronchitis. He noted the woman to be in terrible condition and took note of the tense atmosphere within the Cleary home. He prescribed medication for Bridget and gave her husband strict instructions on how to administer it. She was ill enough that a priest, Father Ryan, was called to the home to deliver communion and last rites.

The decision may have seemed like a normal precaution in a devout Catholic community, but it would later serve as key evidence of how badly Bridget was treated and how seemingly intentionally, her sickness had been allowed to progress. During the later trial, Father Ryan testified that when he arrived at the Cleary home, Bridget was conscious, alive, and agitated. Michael explained to him that though the doctor had prescribed her medicine to treat Bronchitis, he would not give it to her. He told the priest, "People may have some remedy of their own that might do more good than doctor's medicine." Ryan testified that when he arrived at the Cleary home, Bridget was conscious, alive, and agitated. Michael explained to him that though the doctor had prescribed her medicine to treat Bronchitis, he would not give it to her. He told the priest, "People may have some remedy of their own that might do more good than doctor's medicine.

Michael leaves Mary Kennedy and Jack Dunne in charge while he walks four miles to consult another faery doctor in Drangan; this time Cleary is told the only way he can get rid of the faery now is by branding her with a hot poker. Two faerie-hated things were utilised in this method. The combination of fire and iron creates a powerful 10 March.

Bridget gets up and dressed; she sits close to the fire with a blanket around her. Johanna Burke will give evidence that once again Michael

turns the conversation around to faeries. He pulls Budget's head back by her hair and screams at her to admit she is a fairy. Bridget retorts that it was his mother who went away with the fairies and not her. This enrages Michael Cleary so much that he slaps his wife across the face while still retaining his grip on her hair.

Bridget falls to the floor and is too weak to get herself up. She lays on the floor for several minutes until her father helps raise her and helps her back to bed. Michael follows and, still

in a rage, pours the contents of a chamber pot over her. He repeatedly slapped her and beat her on the head and face.
Thursday, 14 March

intense force.   On his return home, he seemed agitated. He had bumped into a neighbour, William Simpson, who had been quite friendly with the Crearys. This he suspects and rumour suggests is his wife's lover. He had overheard the rumours and gossip but had tried to ignore them. When confronted directly, Cleary requests to borrow his gun, but Simpson, sensing something off about Cleary, declines.

Cleary arrives home in a rage; he places the poker into the fire and, asking Dunne, Patrick Bowland, and Mary Kennedy to hold Bridget down, removes the poker, now burning red. At this, both Patrick Bowland and Mary Kennedy refuse, and Bowland attempts to stop Cleary, but a woman and an old man have no chance. Dunne kept reassuring Bowland that this was not their Bridget; this was an old fairy hag they had to get rid of to get their Bridget back.

Cleary pulls back Bridget's head and brands her forehead. Even in her weakened state, Bridget's screams could be heard all over the village. This brought people rushing to the Cleary House, demanding to find out what on earth was going on.

 Bridget is now unconscious, and her father is sobbing bitterly. Michael Cleary and Jack Dunne seek to reassure him that this is not his. Bridget. What they are doing is that Michael refuses to go to the wake, but Mary Kennedy's two sons and Jack Dunne set off to walk the five miles to attend the wake and make Michael Cleary's apology. Bridget can be heard moaning upstairs. Her aunt goes up to her, and Bridget tells her that she is afraid that her husband is going to kill her. She goes on to say that three months earlier he had accused her of going off with the faeries and threatened to burn her. Her aunt and her father were by now extremely fearful, but neither could stand up to Cleary and Jack Dunne. A row suddenly broke out downstairs, and raised voices could be heard. Mary Kennedy goes down to see what the trouble is. She never sees her niece alive again.

March 14

The next day, Thursday, March 14, Michael Cleary went to another herbalist, this time to the locally known "fairy doctor," Dennis Ganey. He purchased more herbs as a "fairy cure." Traditionally a remedy for someone "taken" by fairies is to boil specific herbs in "new" milk (new milk has properties associated with purification), and then the mixture is administered to the patient, which Michael Cleary did. According to the testimony of Johanna Burke, she and William Simpson and his wife Minnie met outside Cleary's door that evening.

The witness asked for admittance, but Michael Cleary said they would not open the door. While they remained outside, they stood at the window. They heard someone inside saying, "Take it, you bitch, or 'witch.'" When the door was opened, the witness went in and saw Dunne and three of Kennedy's sons holding Mrs Cleary down on her bed by her hands and feet, and her husband was giving her herbs and milk in a spoon out of a saucepan. They forced her to take the herbs, and Cleary asked her, "Are you [Bridget] Boland, the wife of Michael Cleary, in the name of God?" She answered it once or twice, and her father asked a similar question.

Michael Cleary [witness thought] then threw a certain liquid on his wife. They put the question to her again, and she [refused] to repeat the words after them. John Dunne then said, "Hold her over the fire, and she will soon answer." Dunne, Cleary, and P. Kennedy then lifted Mrs Cleary off the bed and placed her in a kind of sitting position over the kitchen fire, which was a slow one. Mrs. Cleary had greatly changed. She seemed to be wild and deranged, especially while they were treating her (Folklore 1895, 374).

two earlier doses, encouraged to do so by being threatened with a hot poker, a poker that left a small burn mark on her forehead (Bourke 2000, 91). Fire, particularly applied to iron, is a traditional method of warding off a fairy or frightening a changeling into leaving so that the "real" person can return. The "certain liquid" was urine, traditionally believed to force the changeling to flee; Bridget was repeatedly doused with human urine. The neighbour, Michael Simpson, testified that after the third dose of herbs, while Bridget was still lying on the bed, the men "holding her arms on both sides and her head, they lifted her body and wound it backwards and forwards" (Bourke 2000, 92). This was the third dose of the herbs in milk; earlier, before Johanna Burke and the Simpsons arrived, Bridget had been forced to swallow.

On the morning of Friday, March 15th, Michael Clary fetched the priest, who performed mass in Bridget's bedroom, where Bridget was lying in bed. That night, according to Johanna Burke's testimony, Bridget was dressed and brought to the kitchen, where Johanna says her father, my brother, and myself, and her husband sat at the fire.

They were talking about the fairies, and Mrs. Cleary said to her husband, "Your mother used to go with the fairies, and that is why you think I am going with them." He asked her, "Did my mother tell you that?" She said, "She did; that she gave two nights with them." I made tea and offered Bridget Cleary a cup of it. Her husband got three bits of bread and jam and said she should eat them before she should have supper. He asked her three times: "Are you Bridget Cleary, wife, in the name of God?" She answered twice and ate two pieces of bread and jam. When she did not answer the third time, he forced her to eat the third bite, saying, "If you won't take it, you will go." He flung her on the ground, put his knee on her chest, and one hand on her throat. and forced the bit of bread and jam down her throat, saying, "Swallow it. Is it down? Is it down?" . . . I said, "Mike, let her alone; don't you see it is Bridget that is in it?" meaning that it was Bridget's wife and not the fairy, for he suspected that it was a fairy and not his wife that was there.

Michael Cleary

According to Mary Kennedy's testimony, Michael Cleary said, "Hannah, I believe she is dead." It was at this point that Mary Kennedy saw Michael Cleary reach for the lamp from the table and drench his wife with paraffin oil until she was consumed with flames. James Kennedy testified that when he cried out to Michael Cleary, "For the love of God, don't burn your wife!" Cleary replied, She's not my wife. She's an old deceiver sent in place of my wife. She's been deceiving me for the last seven or eight days and deceived the priest today too, but she won't deceive anyone any more. As I begin it with her, I will finish it with her! .. You'll soon see her go up the chimney! (Bourke 2000, 124).

According to court testimony, at about 2 am the following morning, Michael Cleary asked Johanna Burke's brother, Patrick Kennedy, to help bury Bridget's twisted and partially incinerated corpse. They wrapped the body in a sheet and carried it to a boggy area about a quarter of a mile from Bridget's home. On the 22nd of March, after a week of speculation, newspaper reports, and intensive searching, the Royal Irish Constables discovered the body in a shallow grave. In the intervening time, Michael Cleary, once in the company of his father-in-law and neighbours, spent three nights at the fairy rath at Kylenagranagh, convinced that he would see his wife emerge on a white horse, at which point he would cut her free and rescue her from the fairies, much as Janet rescued Tam Lin.

I am positive that Michael Cleary, and most if not all of the relatives and neighbours who, like Michael, served time for their part in Bridget Cleary's death, genuinely believed that Bridget Cleary had been taken by the fairies.

Kattie Burke, Johanna's young daughter, reported watching Michael Cleary as he picked up his wife and brought her towards the open fire. I won't go into the details of what happened, but this time, it wasn't a threat. Johanna Burke claimed that she tried to escape from the house and call the authorities to stop what was happening, but Michael had locked the door and still had the key in his pocket, swearing that nobody could leave until his real wife returned to him. One of Johanna's brothers, William Kennedy, became faint at the sight of what was happening and had to be revived by his mother with Easter water. Johanna too could soon bear it no longer and ran to the upstairs room. Michael Cleary called up to her. 'Hold your tongue, Hannah." He said. "It is not Bridget I am burning. You will soon see her go up in the chimney." Shortly afterwards, Bridget was dead.

Johanna looked down to the kitchen from the room where she had retreated. Bridget's body was lying face-down on a sheet. on the floor. The people in the house, now that the madness of the last two days was over, seemed at last to understand the seriousness of what they had done. 'In the name of God,' said Mary Kennedy, 'it was the devil that whispered it into his ears.' By now it was daylight on Saturday morning, the 16th of March.

Michael Cleary's actions after his wife's murder were methodical. Johanna Burke watched as he washed the trousers of his light tweed suit. One of Bridget's gold earrings had been left behind, and Michael destroyed it, lest it should be used as evidence against him. He looked for a sack to cover Bridget and left boiled herbs around the house as Jack Dunne had instructed him a few days earlier. Cleary then left the house. He locked the door behind him, shutting in his guests. Then, he went in search of a place about a mile away where he felt he could safely bury Bridget and collected Patrick Kennedy to help.

When they returned to the house, Cleary told the others what was to happen. Johanna Burke, he said, must say that she had prepared Bridget a drink. She had met Bridget at the door upon her return, and Bridget had spat at her and ran out into the night without saying where she was going.

As for himself, Cleary said he would go to Cloneen in the morning and pretend that he was mad. Perhaps this plan might have worked, weak though it was, had it not been for Jack Dunne. Jack had not been at the house on Friday when Bridget was murdered, and before Cleary could carry out his plan to go to Cloneen, Jack arrived at the door. The people inside told Jack that Bridget was missing, and Cleary tried out the story he had just concocted, he hinted to Jack that he thought his wife had left magically and gone to be with the fairies.

Not understanding what had truly happened, Jack Dunne offered to help Cleary search for Bridget. Both men headed to Kylenagranagh Fort, searching the neighbourhood near it.

Eventually, however, Cleary could no longer manage to keep up the deception. He suddenly confessed everything to Jack: "Bridget was burned last night!" Surprisingly, although Jack Dunne had been one of the most superstitious people, and on Thursday it had been him who suggested holding Bridget over the fire, he claimed that he was shocked to hear Cleary's confession and tried to get more details from Michael Cleary about what had happened. But Cleary stuck to his story. The woman he had burned had not truly been Bridget. "She was not my wife," he said. "She was too fine to be my wife. She was two inches taller than my wife."

Dunne urged Cleary to give himself up to the authorities and confess to a priest, so together they walked to the chapel at Drangan. But Fr. Ryan refused to hear Cleary's confession. The priest claimed later that because he seemed so agitated, he was not in a fit state to receive the sacrament of reconciliation. Instead, Fr. Ryan coaxed him outside so that Michael Kennedy could collect him. It seems impossible that the priest wouldn't have known, or at least suspected, that something very serious had happened here. Probably, by refusing to hear confession, Fr. Ryan was simply attempting to prolong his blindness to what had happened and how little he had done to stop it. In any case, he didn't remain ignorant for long in his ignorance. Jack Dunne went up to Fr. Ryan and told him everything: that they had burned Bridget Cleary to death last night and buried her in unconsecrated ground.

Even after hearing this, Fr. Ryan and the parish priest still did not send the whole information to the local police. All they said was that they suspected there was foul play. Still, although they had little to go on, the peelers were quick to take on the case. Walking home from Drangan, Cleary saw a policeman following him. The acting sergeant in the area was a man called Egan, and he met Cleary later on in the day and accompanied him to his house to question him. Cleary continued to maintain that Bridget was missing rather than dead. He told the authorities that Bridget had "left home about twelve o'clock last night." Bridget's father, Pat Boland, still in the house, was tearful. "My daughter will come back to me," he repeated over and over again. Johanna Burke kept up the deception too, telling the police what Cleary had told her to say—that Bridget had spat at her—and ran out through the front door into the night. Without much to go on, Sergeant Egan left the household. He returned later, however, at ten o'clock at night, and found the house deserted. The doors were locked, but Sergeant Egan managed to let himself in through a window in the house.

There, he found Bridget's burned nightdress. All the people who had been involved in Bridget's murder and the cover-up—Cleary himself, Patrick Boland, Jack Dunne, the Kennedys and Burkes, and William Ahearne—were arrested. They were brought to court at Clonmel on March 21st. At this stage, though, nobody had confessed. The prosecutors had only William Simpson's depositions and the false testimony Johanna Burke had given on Cleary's instructions. At this point, all the group could be charged with was wounding Bridget Thursday night through the first exorcism that Simpson had witnessed. Denis Ganey, the herbal doctor who had supplied Cleary with the "medicine," was arrested also, but as he had not forced them to use his concoctions and had no direct part in the exorcism on either night, he was released shortly afterwards. It's a really interesting development that in this case in 1895 the people being tried in the civil court were not the accused witches or fairies, but rather the people who had done the accusing.

The mystery of the missing woman had gripped the locality, but Bridget's husband, father, and cousins continued to keep their silence on what had truly happened to her. Her father, Patrick Boland, even said from the dock, "I have three more persons that can say she was strong the night she went away; she got up and dressed." When led through the streets of Clonmel, the arrested group was greeted with yells and hisses; in the dock though, they did not seem concerned—they chatted together and exchanged pinches of snuff with each other. After the court adjourned, the accused parties were sent to jail.

District Inspector Wansbrough directed the police at Cloneen, Drangan, and Mullinahone "to make a deliberate search" once again for Bridget's body. The following day, Friday, 22nd

March, Sergeant Rogers noticed "some broken thorn bushes freshly cut from a hedge in an angle of a field." And there, under a shallow covering of clay, only a few inches deep, was Bridget's body. Bridget was unclothed, save for her stockings. Her head was enveloped in a sack, and one gold earring hung from her left ear. Although she had been severely burned, her facial features were preserved, and the police knew instantly that it was Bridget they had found. After an inquest in a vacant house nearby, the police buried her, by the light of a lantern, in Cloneen churchyard.

Once her cousin's body had been discovered, Johanna Bourke broke with her part in the deception and finally told the full story of what had happened on that fateful Friday night. The prisoners were returned for trial to the Clonmel Assizes in July, after a prolonged investigation. Michael Cleary was sentenced to twenty years imprisonment, Patrick Kennedy to five, and Jack Dunne to three years. William and James Kennedy received the lighter sentence of eighteen months, while Patrick Boland (Bridget's father) and Michael Kennedy received just six months. Addressing the jury, Judge O'Brien described Bridget as "a young married woman, suspecting no harm, guilty of no offense, virtuous and respectable in all her conduct and all her proceedings." He remarked of the case that it "demonstrates a degree of darkness in the mind, not of one person but of several, a moral darkness, even religious darkness, the disclosure of which had come with surprise on many persons." Indeed, it had. News of the case had spread all across the globe, reaching the Pall Mall Gazette and the

New York Times. People around the world read with horror the lurid details of what had occurred in a small Irish village, an act regarded by many at the time as one of deepest savagery.

. The case also came to feature highly in British discussions of the Home Rule Question. How could this country, remarked British politicians all too eager to keep Ireland in their charge, govern themselves when acts of this nature still occurred? This was not a place of peace or enlightened thought, they said. Bridget Cleary's murder was the most infamous case of supernatural exorcism occurring in Ireland, and she is commonly called "The Last Witch Burned in Ireland" by historical accounts. But her death was not the last of its kind. Just a year later, a man called James Cunningham from Athlone was beaten, tortured, and killed by his father and brothers, who believed that his mental impairments were a sign that he was similarly supernatural or demonic.

Folklore and Fairy

Due to its complexity, folklore does not have a single definition. One definition includes folklore as a historical and cultural process producing and transmitting beliefs, stories, customs, and practices. Folklore is an important part of national identity. It can be studied as an understanding of how people live, giving an insight into people's daily lives. Irish folklore, when mentioned to many people, conjures up images of banshees, fairy stories, leprechauns, and people gathering around, sharing stories. Many tales and legends were passed from generation to generation, as were the ways to celebrate important moments such as marriages, deaths, and birthdays. Folklore came to be regarded as and transformed into a valuable national heritage, particularly fitting for countries, such as Ireland, in search of a strong national identity. English colonization destroyed the nation's long-standing religious and political independence in the sixteenth century. The Great Famine of the 1840s and the deaths and emigration it brought weakened a still powerful Gaelic culture, especially within the rural population.

At the time, intellectuals such as Sir William Wilde expressed concerns about the beauty of traditional beliefs: 'In the state of things, with depopulation the most terrific which any country ever experienced, on the one hand, and the spread of education and the introduction of railroads, colleges, industrial, and other educational schools, on the other—together with the rapid decay of our Irish bardic annals, the vestige of Pagan rites, and the relics of fairy charms preserved—can superstition, or if superstitious belief, can superstitious practices continue to exist?' (Wilde 10-11)

The struggle for home rule (self-government) in Ireland became dire after the Great Famine hit in 1845. Redcliffe N. Salaman, the author of The History and Social Influence of the Potato, announced that the '…state of Ireland in winter 46-47, has convinced me that it would be impossible to exaggerate the horrors of these days or to compare them with anything that has occurred in Europe since the Black Death of

1348. (Salaman 300). The famine had the greatest impact on the Gaeltacht areas, ravishing the rural Gaelic-speaking areas by death and emigration. Traditional Irish culture rapidly declined. The Irish language, oral action, folk customs, and music became minimal as industrialization and English customs replaced the old way of life. One way to keep Gaelic culture alive was through the use of folklore. It was used as a means to cement an Irish national identity in an increasingly changing world. One aspect of Irish folklore is the belief in fairies. This important belief to the Irish people would make headlines around the world in 1895.

Faery Folklore

Faery Lore

Fairy lore is a body of stories, anecdotes, beliefs, and the like that relate to fairies. It usually contains superstitions and stories that were passed down throughout the generations. There are different famous superstitions involving fairy lore. These superstitions mention that fairy forts and hawthorn trees, also known as fairy trees, are the places of residency of fairies. Tampering sites is seen as hugely disrespectful to the fairies. When tampered with, it could be seen as an act of provocation towards these supernatural beings, which would result in unexplainable consequences such as sickness, bad luck, or even death.

There are different types of fairies in Irish fairy lore with different abilities and characteristics. The origin of these Irish fairies could be dated back to the ancient Celtic beliefs of pagan gods and supernatural beings. However, there is no linear path that traces the development of fairy lore in Ireland from its origin. Angela Bourke in her magnificent book The Burning of Bridget Cleary describes fairies as normally invisible, but they are there. They live in the air, under the earth, and in water, and they may be just a little smaller than humans, or so tiny that a grazing cow blows hundreds of them away with every breath (Bouke 33).

Fairies are not humans, but they resemble humans and live lives parallel to theirs, with some significant differences: they keep cows and sell them at fairs; they enjoy whiskey and music; they like gold, milk, and tobacco, but hate iron, fire, salt, and the Christian religion, and any combination of these mainstays of Irish rural culture serves to guard against them. (Bourke 33) Sometimes it is said that there are no women among the fairies. In any case, they steal children and young women, and occasionally young men, and leave withered, cantankerous changelings in their place.

If you offend them (and they can be easily offended), they can bring disease to crops, animals, and humans, but by and large, if treated with neighbourly affection, they mind their own business and even reward favours.

Almost any death, other than a gentle and gradual departure in old age, is open to interpretation as the work of the fairies. A person who spends some time in their company may waste away and die after returning home. Or they may abduct happy, healthy humans, whether children or able-bodied adults and replace them with withered, sickly, evil-tempered changelings, which either live for a while or appear already dead. The changeling is usually an elderly member of the fairies' community.

Changelings' behaviour is often intolerable; however, they take the form of sickly babies who never stop crying or adults who take to their beds, refuse to speak when spoken to, or otherwise conduct themselves in anti-social ways. One way to deal with a changeling is fire. This is said to banish it for good and so force the return of the abducted human.

It is March 1895, and Ireland is calmer and more hopeful than it has been for many years. The young GAA is up on its feet, and the infant Gaelic League is thriving. Aland Bill is finally in sight; home rule remains a hot topic. In South Tipperary, Bridget Cleary, a young, working-class woman, catches a cold. Within weeks, this child of Ballyvadlea, a village of 31 people and nine houses, will make international headlines. The case will be used as evidence of the mental degradation and savagery of the Irish, reasons for the case being erected against Home Rule, against agrarian reform, and much else besides. Papers as far-flung as the New York Times will be reporting that an Irishwoman called Bridget Cleary has been slowly roasted to death because she was, in her relatives' 'bewitched'.

On March 22, 1895, constables found the charred remains of a woman's body in a shallow grave in the corner of a boggy field near Ballyvadlea near Clonmel in Southern Tipperary. The body was severely burned and naked, except for a few remaining scraps of cloth from the victim's undergarments and her black stockings. However, her head was covered with a sack. When they removed this, the police found themselves face to face with the undamaged face of missing Cooper's wife, Bridget Cleary.

Bridget had vanished from her home in the middle of the night some days earlier. However, over a proves, the twenty-six-year-old dressmaker had been suffering from a severe chill that had kept her confined to bed. However, unusual stories about Bridget and her illness were circulating in the district. Many people were murmuring that Bridget Cleary was with the fairies. Several members of Bridget's family, including her husband and father, were charged with her ill-treatment and murder.

The subsequent trial revealed the story of changelings and fairy abductions.

Bridget Cleary lived her whole life in Ballyvadlea, a small townland near Clonmel in southern Ireland. By 1891, the little village consisted of just nine dwellings, housing a population of 31. Like many of the residents, Bridget's father, Patrick Boland, was a local farm labourer. However, he and his wife, who was also called Bridget, ensured that their only daughter and youngest child acquired a good trade and means to support them in their old age.

So, after an education with local nuns, the young Bridget Boland was apprenticed to a dressmaker in Clonmel, eleven miles away.

Bridget's occupation was a good one for a woman of her class and time. It was well-paid for the already pretty teenager to stand out amongst her peers in terms of independence and style. Bridget's looks and individuality meant she attracted plenty of jealous looks—but also plenty of male admirers. So, it was some surprise when Bridget elected to marry at a very early age to a most unlikely man. For in 1887, just as she had completed her apprenticeship, the eighteen-year-old married local Clonmel cooper, Michael Cleary.

Bridget not only lived on a fairy rath, but she also had cause to roam other parts of the countryside associated with the fairies. Since her marriage, Bridget supplemented her dressmaking income with the sales of eggs from hens, the money from which she collected monthly. Part of her egg round took her onto Kylenagranagh Hill, another local fairy fort. The hill was close to the home of one of her customers.

Jack Dunne was a seance—a custodian of the ancient lore. And storyteller. He was also steeped in fairy tales.

March 1895 was bitterly cold, and Bridget caught a chill that confined her to the cottage for several days afterwards. For some reason, the usually healthy woman did not throw off the illness but instead became steadily worse. Various friends and neighbours called around to see how she was. However, when Jack Dunne came to visit, he took one look at Bridget in bed and declared, 'That is not Bridget Boland.'

Michael Cleary, Bridget's husband, overheard. From then onwards, he became convinced that the woman in the bed was not his wife—but a changeling. Ignoring the medicine and diagnosis of the local doctor, Cleary turned to Jack Dunne, who recommended he visit Denis Ganey, a local 'Fairy Doctor.' Ganey did not visit Bridget himself. However, he did give Michael Cleary an herbal mix to be administered to the patient, mixed with new milk.

This cure was a standard one in cases of changelings and was designed to restore the real individual. However, other methods could be used to identify and exorcise a changeling, including harsh, persistent questioning and the threat of fire. All these methods were used on Bridget Cleary on March 14,

1895. Just before ten that night, William Simpson, a local landowner caretaker, and his wife Minnie went to visit Bridget. When Michael Cleary finally allowed them into the cottage, a fearful scene greeted them. Jack Dunne and her cousins Patrick, James, and William were holding a weak and distressed Bridget Cleary on the bed. Bridget's aunt, Mary Kennedy, waited nervously by the door while Michael Cleary forced his wife to take the herb-laced milk.

By now we are told that Bridget was screaming and complaining it was too bitter. However, Cleary held Bridget's mouth shut to force her to swallow, intermittently demanding if she was Bridget Cleary or Bridget Boland, wife of Michael Cleary, in the name of God.

Bridgie is burned. On March 15, the Clearys again had visitors. One was Joanna Burke, who came to see how her cousin was. The most reliable account of the Tipperary horror story—the one held most reliable by the judge—was that of Bridget's cousin, Joanna Burke.

There was then another scream. William Kennedy gathered enough courage to investigate. He quickly returned. 'Bridgie is burned,' he said. Whether by accident or design, Cleary had set his wife's chemo alight. He then poured paraffin over Bridget's body, sat in a chair, and watched her burn.

She's not my wife. She's an old deceiver sent in place of my wife.' Cleary rounded on her relatives: 'You are a dirty set. You would rather have her with the fairies in Kylegranagh [where there was a fairy fort or ringfort] than have her here with me.

That night, Michael Cleary, with the assistance of Mary Kennedy's son, buried Bridget on adjacent land and swore the others to silence. As news spread of Bridget's disappearance, it was plainly said that she had gone with the fairies. But the legend was that she would soon reappear at Kylegranagh Fort, racing along among the fairies on a white horse and that if the men were quick, they could cut the cords tying her to the horse and that she would stay with them.

Meanwhile, the police had acquired sworn statements from both William Simpson and Joanna Burke, and on March 23rd, Simpson led RIC men to the shallow grave about a quarter-mile from Cleary's house. They found Bridget Cleary's body, naked, apart from a few scraps of rags stuck to her flesh and a pair of black stockings. Five days later, she was buried under cover of darkness without a priest, her body placed in a common car, escorted by four police constables. All ten people who had been in the house in the days surrounding the murder were arrested, but only the men involved were given sentences ranging from six months to twenty years. Court records

The trial gives remarkable detail from those who became witnesses, including Bridget's cousin Johanna Burke and her ten-year-old daughter Katie. Court records show Michael Cleary was sentenced to twenty years for his part in the murder and, on his release, went to Liverpool and then to Canada.

Conclusion Bridget's death shows the religious, political, and sociological attitudes in nineteenth-century Ireland. Contemporary newspaper reports of the murder case of Bridget Cleary gauge the political reaction at a time of unrest.

The unionist Dublin Evening Mail drew comparisons between the death of Bridget Cleary and the Home Rule question, contending that the people of Ballyvadlea were lawless and considered the law of the land an English one to be ignored. Across the political divide, there were differences in the tone and content of reports. While folklore was an important element in creating a distinct Irish identity, it was also used to highlight the 'barbarism' of the Irish peasantry. Although this was a changing case where fire was used in a ritualistic way, the newspapers referred to it as witch burning. Linking the Cleary case to the burning of witches during the early modern period was a clever journalistic ploy to attract readers. In the popular imagination,

Witches were often hanged rather than burned to death, just as had been. 'Witch Burning Case' (Glasgow Herald, July 5th, 1895) was far more catchy for international headlines and bylines than 'fairy burning'. For such reasons, her story has endured and still captures the popular imagination today. The truth that emerged subsequently was a toxic mix of fairy folklore, illness, superstition, social mores, and the ever-present suspicion of women with a mind and means of their own. Works Cited Bourke, Angela.

Michael and Jack Dunne.

So what could turn a religious, law-abiding Irishman to murder his wife in front of their family and friends? The man, Michael Cleary, did not believe he was committing murder. He did not believe he was in any way harming his beloved wife, Bridget. To Michael, his actions were the last effort to save his wife from a terrible fate. He believed, against the advice of doctors and priests, that the creature he was killing was not his Bridget. He believed it was a fairy—a changeling masquerading as Bridget—while the real Mrs Cleary remained trapped in another realm. In the days leading up to the brutal attack, the Cleary home had dissolved into chaos. Bonds of trust between family, friends, church officials, and medical professionals were pushed to their limit. Michael Cleary became a startling example of what can happen when religious vigour, old-world superstition, and evolving ideas about the roles of women collide.

To understand Michael Cleary's crime, you have to understand what fueled his impossible beliefs. The world was changing for Ireland in 1895, and that terrifying frontier of progress broke apart a young couple's marriage and a community's trust. Bridget Boland married Cooper Michael Cleary in August of 1887. She was a bright, lovely, talented young woman with charm enough to win her any husband she wanted. The man she wanted, Michael, was a working-class man and a devout Catholic. As a cooper, he made barrels, wooden casks, and other goods created from local timber. Michael had been trained as an apprentice to make his wares by hand, a skill that was quickly becoming overshadowed by the industrial boom and more efficient means of creating and distributing products. Even so, it seems Michael did not have a difficult time making a match with the vibrant Bridget Boland. Their marriage was one of mutual love—Bridget seeing a worthy and loving partner in Michael, and Michael seeing a sweet and virtuous girl in Bridget.

From all accounts, the early days of their marriage were normal. Michael was a hard worker with a determination to provide for his beautiful new bride and make a name for himself. While Bridget had a good deal of care and respect for her husband, she was not satisfied with the traditional "woman's work" in the home. Bridget took up work as a dressmaker's apprentice, a decision that kindled a small bit of friction between the couple. Working women may have been more common at this time than they had been in decades past, but it was a concept still shunned by more conservative households. This was especially true for the traditional Catholic families of Ireland. Michael was not making enough to support himself and Bridget in the way he wanted, but he was still adamant that a wife should stay home—not worry herself about a career outside of the home. This notion was problematic. Bridget's skill as a dressmaker offered a possibility for the family to live comfortably, if not very well off. She had no intention of letting her abilities go to waste in the interest of satisfying her husband's old-fashioned sensitivity.

Not long after their marriage, Bridget returned to her parents' house in Ballyvadlea. Michael stayed behind in Clonmel to finish up his current affairs as a cooper.

Michael wanted desperately to prove to Bridget he was capable of fulfilling the long-accepted role as a husband and sole breadwinner. Unbeknownst to him, Bridget had expanded her career since leaving Clonmel. She continued her dressmaking after purchasing a Singer sewing machine. At the time, the Singer model was state-of-the-art. It offered women a chance to produce quickly and venture into the world of business. The same technological boom that was making men like Michael obsolete was giving their wives more opportunities outside of the home. Michael wasn't the only man in Ireland bothered by the uptick in women's professions, but the prospect of not having to scrape by in poverty seemed to win out in many households.

. Unfortunately for Michael, dressmaking was not the only job Bridget had taken on. She bought and kept her flock of chickens and made decent money selling the eggs to friends and neighbours. This meant taking long walks in rain or shine across the moors to customers. If there is a defining detail to mark where the tables began to turn between Michael and Bridget, her daily trek across the moors sparked the fire that would turn into a full-on blaze of superstition. The Irish moors, much like the English moors, were thought to be more than just vast empty wetlands. These flat expanses of fog and marsh were the subject of centuries of Irish folklore. Thought to hide entryways into the realm of the fairies, these desolate spaces were filled with tales of dangerous creatures and mischievous tricksters. Irish children were raised to be wary of them. Those who held tight to the old Irish superstitions and folk beliefs thought it possible for someone to disappear into the fog and be spirited away by unnatural creatures.

Michael Cleary was one of these believers. Fairies of old Irish mythology were not kind, flower-wearing creatures who sprinkled magic dust and granted wishes. Irish fairies were tricksters, kidnappers, instigators, and monsters. In some legends, fairies destroyed homes and crops when they felt insulted. In others, they would spirit away young virgins to corrupt their purity. The most famous fairy tale was much more frightening. The story of the changelings was a very real concern in old-world Ireland.

Legend has it that if a loved one, adult or child, began to behave out of character, it was likely they were not their loved one at all. These changes indicated the presence of a changeling—a fairy sent to take the place of a human while the real human was kidnapped to the fairy realm. Changeling trials were, for a time, a popular branch of witch hysteria in old Europe. It was believed these creatures were evil, and casting them out of the community was the only way to restore virtue and balance. Unfortunately, the methods for removing a changeling were often violent and dangerous.

Suspected changelings could be beaten, burned, held over fire, or underwater, and in some cases poisoned by concoctions of deadly plants such as foxglove. By the 1890s, much of Ireland had turned from belief in these horrific methods. The Catholic Church even began to dissuade followers from giving in to the hysteria of such superstitions and the dangers they could bring. Still, some refused to let go of the fairy realm. There were still men and women believed to be "fairy doctors"—individuals skilled in providing medical treatment when a supernatural creature or ailment was the cause. Bridget's cousin Jack Dunne was one of these so-called doctors. Those who believed in the dangers of the fairy realm relied on men like Dunn for help but also kept an arsenal of old folk protections on hand to circumvent the possibility of a supernatural attack.

There were safety precautions one could take to avoid the misfortune of fairies. Many learned to leave them bowls of milk and sugar to keep them satisfied. Others would leave out small gifts and offerings in hopes of appeasing the fairies and avoiding their ire. You could also adorn your home with iron objects, as the belief that fairies were repelled by iron was commonly accepted. Above all these things, the most important way to avoid a tangle with the fairies was to stay out of the moors and far away from the fairy rings.

Fairy rings were circles made of natural items and thought to function as a doorway to the fairy realm. A naturally occurring circle of mushrooms, trees, or even rocks was thought to be a dangerous place. Many avoided them altogether, but some brave souls went to the fairy rings on purpose in hopes of summoning the creatures to ask for a favour, or more morbidly, speak to the dead. Some of the supposed fairy rings had much more explainable and logical origins. Many were later proven to be the remnants of long-forgotten man-made structures that had eroded over time to resemble circular imprints of stone and other leftover material. Ballyvadlea had many of these old circles, which slowly, little by little, townsfolk had begun to disregard. When Michael eventually left Clonmel to join his wife in Ballyvadlea, he was horrified to learn of Bridget's professional advancement. The realisation that her new business also took her on frequent trips through the dreaded moors shook Michael to his core and planted a seed of paranoia that had not existed in their marriage before. To make matters worse, after the death of Bridget's mother, the couple assumed care of her elderly father, Patrick Boland.

Once a labourer, Patrick was able to provide the family with fine accommodations in a labour village. It was said he acquired the nicest house in the village for his small family.

But it wasn't cunning or luck that afforded Boland the lovely new home. The other families in the village had no interest in the house, many rejecting the opportunity to live there. The aversion came from a widely accepted local legend—the Boland house was built on the site of a fairy ring. The labour village was full of older and less educated families, making it a community still primed for fear in the old legends. This information haunted Michael. His wife's differing views were difficult to accept, but their proximity to dangerous fairy rings gave him the perfect excuse for Bridget's behaviour.

It is Michael likely began their fairy folk were to blame for his troubles from the moment he arrived in Ballyvadlea. His firm belief in the superstitious legends of old and devout Catholicism made him feel as though he were a champion of righteousness in a world clouded by dark forces. These beliefs grew stronger as Bridget flourished, mixing with his mounting frustration of not finding steady work while his wife became more successful. A deadly storm was brewing inside Michael Cleary. In March of 1895, Bridget went out to make her normal rounds, delivering to customers. She intended to check in on her cousin, Jack Dunne, who lived across the moors when her work was done and returned home afterwards in a foul mood that day. Still struggling to find work, as well as jealous and confused by his wife's success, it is believed that Michael and Bridget fought that morning over baseless accusations of adultery.

Michael had a lot of time on his hands, and most of it was spent tormenting himself over what his wife was up to when she was out of the house. He worried about the fairies and became enraged and embarrassed that Bridget was effectively the family's provider. Even if Bridget suggested Michael join her on the delivery route, he refused.

To Michael Cleary, the only thing worse than staying home while your wife worked was working with her in a business she created. Michael believed Bridget was changing. He may not have been completely wrong. Reports from some who knew the couple claimed he criticised her hours away from home, methods of prayer, and choice in clothing—even taking issue with the undergarments she chose to wear. Michael's idea of a proper wife was set in stone, and there was no room for a woman looking to change and progress. As difficult as their home life was becoming, there is no evidence to suggest that Bridget was interested in anything other than finding balance with her troubled husband.

She was an evolving independent woman, yes, but she still held tight to her Catholic faith and believed in the sanctity of her marriage. Bridget decided not to back down and bend to Michael's will. As far as she was concerned, he was more than welcome at her side. If he would prefer to sulk at home all day, that was his choice. In the days leading up to her murder, Bridget had fallen ill. She was suffering from a sore throat and terrible coughing fits that were made worse by long treks through cold wetlands. Still, illness would not keep Bridget from her work.

The day she set out to visit Jack Dunne, Bridget's symptoms seemed to have escalated. She became disoriented while wandering through the moors and was said to have been lost for several hours before stumbling home. Her father and Michael were present when she finally arrived. Her father was concerned and urged her to get to bed, but Michael was completely horrified at her condition. The sick woman was confused, fevered, and clearly in need of medical attention. The stuttering, sickly woman struggling to stand up on her own did not resemble Bridget Cleary. Michael knew

To most, these would be clear signs of a severe illness. To the frustrated and suppressed Mr Cleary, the symptoms were signifiers of something else. If Michael had been harbouring any deep desire to harm Bridget, this had given him the perfect excuse. Michael and Patrick sent for a doctor, though Michael believed he already knew what was wrong with his wife. The woman had returned from a known fairyland, acting strangely and almost inhuman. This couldn't be Bridget. Without input from Patrick, Michael sent for another person to diagnose Bridget's condition—her fairy doctor cousin, Jack Dunne.

There are conflicting reports as to whether or not Michael initially sent for a medical doctor in the first place or simply told his father-in-law he had.

At this period in Ireland, most villages had few, if any, doctors. If someone fell ill, a doctor had to be sent. Thurney could take precious days, which it did in Bridget's case. Some neighbours believed Michael had sent for Jack instead, only relenting to call for a real doctor at the anger and insistence of Patrick. In either case, Jack Dunne arrived and examined Bridget. His diagnosis confirmed Michael's superstitious fears. The woman in his home was not even a real woman; it was an evil fairy changeling. Jack and Michael got to work planning folk cures to dispel the changeling.

If Patrick was sceptical at first, the urging of both his nephew and son-in-law eventually swayed him. Within a day, he had decided to help the other men with their nonsensical mission. Patrick would claim he truly had begun to believe Bridget was in danger. The medical doctor arrived days later and diagnosed Bridget with a severe case of bronchitis. He noted the woman to be in terrible condition and took note of the tense atmosphere within the Cleary home. He prescribed medication for Bridget and gave her husband strict instructions on how to administer it. She was ill enough that a priest, Father Ryan, was called to the home to deliver communion and last rites.

The decision may have seemed like a normal precaution in a devout Catholic community, but it would later serve as key evidence of how badly Bridget was treated and how seemingly intentionally her sickness had been allowed to progress. During the later trial, Father Ryan testified that when he arrived at the Cleary home, Bridget was conscious, alive, and agitated. Michael explained to him that though the doctor had prescribed her medicine to treat Bronchitis, he would not give it to her. He told the priest, "People may have some remedy of their own that might do more good than doctor's medicine." Father Ryan was unsettled by Cleary's words and encouraged him to follow the doctor's orders and not be overcome by fairy mythology.

Ryan believed that medical care, not magic, was in Bridget's best interest. Michael did not agree. Father Ryan left the home that evening, having been unable to convince Michael. According to changing mythology, once a loved one has been taken, there are only nine days to save them. If left unrescued past the ninth day, they are the fairies forever. This meant that Michael was on a deadline if he ever wanted to see his wife again. Doctor'sThe doctor'sand the priest's urging meant little to him. Michael believed that these other treatments were wasting time, allowing the unholy creature to exist longer in his wife's place. As days ticked by, Bridget was defiant as as ever. Being close to death did not stop the willful young woman from standing her ground. No matter the torture, she refused to admit any wrongdoing. Michael's methods of "treatment" became more severe, an observation that began to disturb some of the friends and family who visited the house in those days.

Patrick was among the disturbed, eventually believing the changeling must be gone and Bridget had already returned. Sadly, there was little the loving but frail father could do to help his daughter. The old man was no match for Michael, whose anger, frustration, and tension had come to a boiling point. To make matters worse, Jack actively fueled Michael's mounting paranoia, offering another extreme "cure" each time one seemed to fail.

During these supernatural treatments, the sick woman was held down and forced to drink a tonic of urine. When that did not yield results that satisfied Michael, he tormented her with items heated by the fire. As Bridget struggled, Michael shouted at her to submit and confess to being a changeling. Bridget held her ground, even as the consequences became more deadly. Bridget's attending loved ones assisted Michael in many of the initial attacks. Both her father and cousin were reported to have helped hold her down when the urine tonic was used—despite the horrified woman screaming and pleading through a Bronchitis-riddled throat.

By the time Bridget was a few days into her illness, her family had begun to doubt there was a supernatural cause at all. It became difficult to justify the cruelty, especially when the victim was a person—at least physically—they had known and cared for. It is unclear exactly why her family did not put a stop to Michael's behaviour. On the final day of Bridget's life, Michael is reported to have demanded that she admit to being a fairy impostor one last time, a deadly amount of anger rising within him. Bridget, though badly beaten and still sick, refused. No matter how much Michael screamed and threatened, Bridget was determined to stand her ground. In a fit of rage, Michael lifted Bridget by her neck and threw her onto the stones in front of the fireplace. He then poured lamp oil over her and set her nightgown on fire. Bridget's father and other family members witnessed the event.

The poor woman, who was still recovering from her real sickness, was burned in front of an audience whom she had once believed loved her. Whether or not Bridget was burned alive is still a point of debate. The court was unable to determine if Bridget died when her head hit the stone floor or if she was killed by the fire, but the result was clear—Bridget Cleary had been murdered in cold blood at the hands of her husband. Witnesses gave varied reports as to what happened next in the Cleary home.

On March 22, 1895, her body was discovered in a shallow grave after neighbours reported she had been missing for several days. Ten people were arrested for the crime, including Michael. Of the ten, all but Michael were freed of the charge of murder, but four were convicted of "wounding." The trial gained international attention, prompting the media to dub Bridget "the last witch burned in Ireland." Some news outlets used the case as justification for terrible Irish stereotypes. As if the tragic end to her life was not enough, Bridget became a cautionary tale meant to insult her own. The media claimed that her murder was proof of the Irish being an uneducated and backward people incapable of governing themselves without descending into superstitious chaos.

The coverage added insult to injury and, more often than not, failed to give any respect to the young woman who had been senselessly cut down in the prime of her life. Michael showed no remorse for the killing. Those present at his trial were horrified to hear witnesses claim that even as her body burned, he continued to shout it was only a changeling, and the creature's death would bring his wife back to him.

The arresting officers would testify that Michael was incredulous during his arrest. He seemed completely certain Bridget would step back through the fairy ring any day now and the entire mess would be cleared up. Fairies, magic, and the evil beyond the veil were all real to Michael Cleary. He was convinced he had done his community a favour by dispelling a dangerous force. With or without fairy lore, that is likely exactly what Michael believed. Michael Cleary spent fifteen years in prison on the charge of manslaughter. There is no evidence he ever apologised for or admitted to killing his wife. After his release, Michael is recorded to have immigrated to Canada, where he disappeared from public record. What happened in the Cleary home during that terrible spring of 1895 will never be completely revealed. Why did Bridget's family go along with Michael? Why did they stand by for so long? How did one man murder his wife in front of a group of people who supposedly cared for her without significant challenge? Cleary was certainly a slightly unusual woman by the standards of the time, but there are no facts to point to anything untoward. Although witches, changelings, and assorted superstitions were common cultural beliefs at the time, and as a child, she went regularly to the Faery Fort nearby.

It was here that Bridget would whisper her secrets to the Faeries and speak of her hopes and longings for the future. She was the only girl in a family of three brothers and both of her parents.

She didn't make friends easily and was described as a little aloof by some of her neighbours. Certainly, before the death of her mother, she was regarded as a most level-headed woman.

Faery Rings and Faery Mounds.

The Sidhe Mounds.

Ballyvadlea had many of these old circles, which slowly, little by little, townsfolk had begun to disregard. When Michael eventually left Clonmel to join his wife in Ballyvadlea, he was horrified to learn of Bridget's professional advancement. The realisation that her new business also took her on frequent trips through the dreaded moors shook Michael to his core and planted a seed of paranoia that had been encouraged by Jack Dunne and had not existed in their marriage before. To make matters worse, after the death of Bridget's mother, the couple assumed care of her elderly father, Patrick Boland.

Once a labourer, Patrick was able to provide the family with fine accommodations in a labour village. It was said he acquired the nicest house in the village for his small family. But it wasn't cunning or luck that afforded Boland his lovely new home. The other families in the village had no interest in the house, many rejecting the opportunity to live there. The aversion came from a widely accepted local legend—the Boland house was built on the site of a fairy ring.

But their proximity to dangerous fairy rings gave him the perfect excuse for Bridget's behaviour. Michael likely began to suspect their fairy folk were to blame for his troubles from the moment he arrived in Ballyvadlea. His firm belief in the superstitious legends of old and devout Catholicism made him feel as though he were a champion of righteousness in a world clouded by dark forces. These beliefs grew stronger as Bridget flourished, mixing with his mounting frustration of not finding steady work while his wife became more successful. A deadly storm was brewing inside Michael Cleary. Bridget Cleary was not the only one murdered by her husband at this time. Apart from that, reports and inquest verdicts can still be seen on the Irish court database. Though it is considered one of the very worst cases.

Faery Lore lived on in Ireland largely until the Gaelic Revival because of the fairy women and fairy men—wise, older, usually disabled individuals who prescribed herbal cures, told the stories of Ireland's rich mythological past and provided guidance to those dealing with the diseases and symptoms lore associated with fairy interference.

Bridget Cleary's cousin, Jack Dunne, who helped Michael Cleary administer the herbs boiled in new milk to Bridget, was one such individual. Though not the fairy man that Cleary went to for herbs—that was Denis Ganey—Dunne was a respected orator, known for his storytelling skill, and made a living at that.

 This woman died over days by people who were supposed to love her. The magnitude of the level of cruelty while onlookers did nothing. These individuals weren't the sole authorities in Victorian Ireland. The agents of Irish modernity were increasingly visible in all corners of the island. University-trained doctors, the Royal Irish Constabulary—a modern police force created in 1822 to survey the provinces of Ireland—and, of course, the expanding legion of Catholic priests throughout Ireland.

These various entities worked in concert and in opposition to control and administer to the people of rural Ireland to replace and preserve the heritage of Fae and superstition. Sarah: Charles Dickens and countless other scholars of the Victorian period argued that literacy and Victorian literature killed the superstitious belief in fairies in the United Kingdom. Generally, the rise of print media is associated with the modernization of the middling and educated Anglophone world.

Lady Augusta Gregory, WB Yeats, Lady Wilde, and, in the 1930s, the Folklore Commission of the Free State of Ireland—among others—collected the mythologies, legends, and fairy tales of Celtic Ireland. They preserved those stories in a world otherwise designed to wipe out pagan superstition. They published the collected lore in journals, poetry collections, books, children's magazines, and shillings monthlies, consumed extensively by the increasingly literate public. Ave: This isn't to suggest that reading about fairies in children's books means that adults grow up to believe their sick wives are changelings. That's not the correlation that Sumpter is making, and it's not the correlation we're making. Instead, what is interesting is that the facilitators of the Gaelic Revival, the people who preserved the cultural heritage of fairy tales, were upper-class, educated, and largely urban elite. Victorian men and women. They were not remotely like the people they interviewed to collect those stories, and in their romantic narratives of the quaint Celtic fringe folk, they propagated a particular vision of rural Ireland: illiterate, superstitious, backwards, barbarians.

Johanna Burke testified that she told Bridget she didn't believe in fairies and certainly didn't believe Bridget was a changeling. Michael Cleary was a literate craftsman. He apprenticed as a cooper in Clonmel, the 'big city' (relatively speaking), about 16 miles from Bridget's hometown of Ballyvadlea in County Tipperary. He met Bridget there when he was working, and she was apprenticing in a dressmaker's shop. Bridget spent four years in Clonmel learning her craft and bought a sewing machine of her own to take back to Ballyvadlea.

Michael Cleary's appalling crime and his insistence that he did so because he believed she was a fairy was further evidence for the British newspaper-reading public that the Irish were unfit to rule themselves.

Johanna Burke testified that she told Bridget she didn't believe in fairies and certainly didn't believe Bridget was a changeling. Michael Cleary was a literate craftsman. He apprenticed as a cooper in Clonmel, the 'big city' (relatively speaking), about 16 miles from Bridget's hometown of Ballyvadlea in County Tipperary. He met Bridget there when he was working, and she was apprenticing in a dressmaker's shop. Bridget spent four years in Clonmel learning her craft and bought a sewing machine of her own to take back to Ballyvadlea.

Both Bridget and Michael would've been National School educated, Bridget perhaps to the official leaving age of 14, after which she took up her apprenticeship. Sarah: They married in the mid-1880s, and for the first four years of their union, she lived in Ballyvadlea with her ailing mother and elderly father; he lived in Clonmel, visiting her on the weekends. After her mother passed away, Bridget, Michael, and Bridget's father, Patrick Boland, applied for and were granted tenants of the only new-build labourer's cottage in Ballyvadlea. Michael moved in and started making barrels for the local dairy. This took some smart finagling—these government-subsidised housing projects were to be reserved for farm labourers, and only Bridget's elderly father qualified.

They used his technical designation to secure the finest home in Ballyvadlea. As a pair, Bridget and Michael Cleary were quite well-off, compared to their neighbours and family members. Bridget's dressmaking income and egg sales set her starkly above the other women in her community, including her cousin, Johanna Burke, the Queen's witness in the case against Michael Cleary. It seems unlikely that an educated, skilled, smart man like Michael Cleary would buy into fairy lore.

Angela Bourke suggests that his dishevelled mental state—worry over his ailing wife and the feverish things she was saying, lack of sleep and adequate food intake, and walking all over Tipperary in search of help for Bridget—was exploited by resentful and superstitious family members.

It was Jack Dunne who suggested that a fairy cure was needed and not to heed the doctor. The doctor's drunkenness probably didn't help to inspire confidence. But the Cleary's relative prosperity in a deeply impoverished region certainly didn't help their situation. And there's also the possibility of some underlying currents of resentment—after all, Bridget wasn't merely rising above her kin. Her economic ventures and the couple's childlessness, while freeing economically, were likely a source of strain, possibly even resentment, between the two. Undoubtedly, Michael blamed his wife for the failure to conceive a child. None or any of these symptoms alone might be cause for wife murder, but certainly, the convergence of these conditions created a very dangerous situation for Bridget Cleary.

Bridget Cleary's story is also unique in that, while she wasn't the only suspected fairy murdered in nineteenth-century Ireland, she was the only adult. Stories about children being taken by the fairies—babies dying suddenly of wasting illnesses or children murdered by terrified parents—were mental leaps that allowed people to exist in a world of high infant mortality, poverty, and sickness.

But Bridget was a grown woman. The continuous accusation that she was a changeling is the strangest and most suspicious element of the case. Sir William Wilde—Oscar's father—was a doctor who studied both fairy folklore and catalogued the illnesses of his patients in the Irish countryside. The 19th-century newspapers are also peppered with stories of children "fairy struck"—the Morning Post reported in 1836 that "Ann Roche, an old woman of very advanced age, was indicted for the murder of Michael Leahy, a young child, by drowning him in the flesh. This heartbreaking case turned out to be a murder committed under the delusion of the grossest superstitions.

The child, though four years old, could neither stand, walk, nor speak—it was thought to be fairy-struck. Disturbing, deeply sad, and complicated in their own right, the murder of children who were suspected of being changelings is consistent with a fairly standard fairy tale: changelings almost universally took the place of children.

The deliberate cruelty handed out to this child by his grandmother sends shivers down the spine. And all because he was so badly disabled. When his mother died, his father bundled him up and practically threw him at his grandmother. Who was in shock? The last time she had seen him, he was a healthy, happy little boy, and his mother was in good health. Now he was hidden away like some dark secret, and instead of looking to the father for answers, it was easier to blame the faeries.

Back to Bridget What is most disturbing to me is the bystander element of this story. Johanna Burke was not the only one present as Michael Cleary murdered his wife. According to the court testimonies, Patrick and James Kennedy were napping in Bridget's father's room—not far from the commotion in the kitchen by any means if they were even really sleeping there—and Mary Kennedy was sleeping in Cleary's bed. But Patrick Boland, Johanna Burke, and William Kennedy were all in the kitchen when Michael attacked his wife for the final time. Johanna says she cried out, telling him to stop—but made no move to stop him. William, a strapping and tall 21-year-old man, did nothing to pull the violent man off of his cousin.

Perhaps they were stunned by the explosion. Perhaps they, in some deeper part of their subconscious, believed she was a fairy. Perhaps they wished her ill.

Everyone behaved so bizarrely, unfeelingly, on that terrible Friday night. When Michael stood over his wife's burned body, he told the (reportedly) shocked family members present that it was done now, and Bridget would come to the local fairy fort on a white horse, and that they had to be there to free her from the fairies with an iron knife.

Patrick Kennedy helped Michael Cleary bury his wife in a shallow grave, wearing nothing but a sack over her head and her black stockings. He convinced a bewildered William Kennedy to go with him that very night to wait outside the ringfort for three nights. Surely, he told them, she'd appear by the end of three nights.

Of course, she did not appear. She was dead, first shoved hastily into an 18-inch hole and later buried quietly by the RIC. in Clonen, under the cover of darkness, on Wednesday, March 27, a charred corpse.

In early investigations, people like Johanna Burke swore to the local constables that Bridget got up and walked out of the house when she was put to the fire. Most perpetuated Cleary's delusion/cover story. As early as Saturday, the 16th, there were rumours of foul play regarding Bridget's disappearance.

William Simpson went to the police on Monday, March 18, and when the constables went for a second round of questions, Johanna Burke changed her tune and gave a new statement. On March 21st, those connected to the murder were arrested. When the Royal Irish Constabulary found her body on March 22, they'd already arrested 11 people: Johanna Burke; her mother, Mary Kennedy; her sons, William, Patrick, Michael, and James Kennedy; Bridget's father, Patrick Boland; Jack Dunne; the herb doctor, Denis Ganey; a 16-year-old boy who'd been present at the milk fiasco; and, of course, Michael Cleary. Ganey was soon released when it was clear he had no direct involvement in the murder. Johanna Burke, as we've said, turned Queen's witness and was granted immunity from prosecution.

The jury, after three days of testimonies nearly a month of evidence-collecting by the RIC and just 40 minutes of deliberation, returned with guilty verdicts for all nine remaining prisoners. They strongly recommended Patrick Boland, Michael Kennedy, and Mary Kennedy to mercy.

They found Patrick Kennedy most guilty, besides Michael Cleary, for his role in the disposal of the body—he got 5 years imprisonment. Jack Dunne got 3 years, less than the 5 the judge thought he deserved on account of his age. William and James Kennedy got 18 months. Patrick Boland and Michael Kennedy got 6 months imprisonment, and Mary Kennedy got none.

About Michael Cleary, the judge delivered quite a pronouncement. "The short of the matter was that he burned his wife alive. [I do] not know that these medicines the prisoner procured or those herbs were intended for the cure," but the judge could also not say whether or not Michael Cleary was mad because there hadn't been a lengthy inquest into that line of thought. All the same, the judge continued, "the fact that the prisoner inflicted upon the woman whom he swore before the altar to cherish and protect—that he took her life away [in what was] generally regarded as the most cruel and painful of human afflictions, by burning her alive.

She was not dead at the time he threw the paraffin oil on her, and his wicked hand sent her to another world in the very prime of her life—a young woman who confessed to him her affections and her life, and he most wantonly and most cruelly and most wretchedly betrayed her.

All the same, the judge found himself doubting the clarity of the case enough that he stopped short of the extreme sentence. He did not doubt Michael Cleary's guilt, but he did doubt Cleary's sanity in the case. And so he sentenced Cleary. to 20 years of penal servitude. According to the Irish Examiner, during the delivery of the sentence, "the prisoner wept bitterly. He seemed very agitated and left the dock, wringing his hands.

The Danger of Faeries

Fairies were dangerous. Not believing in them was dangerous. Not to respect them or take them seriously was dangerous—hence all the carefully euphemistic or indirect names one used in speaking of them, from "the Gentry" to "the Good People," "themselves," "the fair folk," and "the people of peace," through to the charming Welsh phrase beneath û mamma, or "such as have deserved their mother's blessing." Fairies stole your children. They made you or your animals sick, sometimes unto death. They could draw the life, or essence, out of anything, from milk or butter through to people. Their powers, as we have seen, were almost limitless, not only demonic but even godlike in scale and scope.

While ordinary people still believed this less than a century ago, the educated also believed it in the era of witch persecution. Witches did these kinds of things, and fairies or fairyland were quite often referenced in their trials. Although Joan of Arc was tried as a heretic rather than a witch, the latter association naturally clung to such an unusual woman, and it is notable that in 1431 her interrogators took an interest in the "fairy tree" around which Joan had played in her childhood in Domrémy. In the Protestant camp, Calvin later emphasised how "the Devil works strange illusions by fairies and satyrs." In early modern Sicily, one distinct type of witch was the female "fairy doctor," the phrase donna di fuori ("woman from outside") meaning either "fairy" or "fairy doctor." Here, inquisitors encouraged people, including suspected witches, to equate fairy and witch beliefs. In 1587, they were especially interested in one Laura di Pavia, a poor fisherman's wife who claimed to have flown to Fairyland in Benevento, Kingdom of Naples.

In many cases, educated witch-believers saw fairies and fairyland as sources of dark power for witches.

Lizanne Henderson lists 38 Scottish witch trials (1572—1716) featuring references to fairy beliefs, including that of Isobel Strathaquin (Aberdeen, 1597), accused of using skills which she "learnt... of an elf-man who lay with her." At the 1616 trial of Katherine Caray, the accused spoke of meeting not only "a great number of fairy men" on the Caithness hills at sunset but "a master man"—a figure which in this context could have been seen as "the King of the Fairies" or "the Prince of Darkness."

After a Scottish girl, Christian Shaw, suffered hysterical fits in 1696, the ensuing trial featured a veritable cauldron of lurid evidence, from a mysterious black man with cold hands through to the eating of "a piece of unchristened child's liver" and a charm of blood and stones used by one Margaret Fulton, a reputed witch whose "husband had brought her back from the fairies."

Like witches, fairies were powerful, uncanny, and unpredictable. And like witches, vampires, or any of the world's numerous magical figures, fairies were scapegoats. They could be blamed for almost anything.

Ann Jeffreys.

One particular case of demonised fairies is so intriguing that it merits a little space to itself. Its protagonist was Ann Jefferies, a maidservant of the Pitt family at St. Teath, Cornwall. In 1645, aged nineteen, Ann was "one day knitting in an arbour in our garden" when "there came over the garden hedge to her six persons of a small stature, all clothed in green, which she called fairies, upon which she was so frightened, that she fell into a kind of a convulsion fit." So related was the bookseller and printer Moses Pitt fifty years later, having been six at the time of Ann's encounter.

What followed looks in many ways like the career of a fairy doctor. Ann seemed to suffer some kind of neurosis about food and allegedly took none from the family for several months, claiming that the fairies themselves fed her. Ann presently cured Mrs Pitt's leg after a bad fall merely by stroking it and soon became so famous that numerous people flocked to the house for cures from as far south as Land's End and as far north as London. All cures seemed to be done purely by touch, without medicines. Ann showed psychic ability, knowing of her visitors before they arrived. Moses himself never saw the fairies, but his mother and sister both did.

This case is already interesting for the way that it echoes those of other fairy doctors, despite the Pitt family (and other affluent patients from London) having no concept of such figures.

The element of danger initially seems brief, being limited to Ann's fear at the first encounter. But presently local ministers began to insist that the fairies were "evil spirits" and that the whole affair was "a delusion of the Devil." A warrant appeared; Pitt's family and Ann were questioned by local authorities; and magistrate John Tregeagle had An locked up—first in Bodmin Jail and next in his own house, where he kept her without food. Although witchcraft was not explicitly mentioned, it is hard not to suspect that this was on people's minds. The instability of the Civil War may have further aggravated such fears: the female prophet Anna Trapnel sparked controversy in January 1645, and Sarah Wight had a similar effect in the weeks after February 1647.

Like witches, fairies were powerful, uncanny, and unpredictable. And like witches, vampires, or any of the world's numerous magical figures, fairies were scapegoats. They could be blamed for almost anything, from human deaths to mass famine. In one sense, the fairy as a scapegoat was potentially a good thing. For fairies, real or not, could not be harmed. Women taken for witches certainly could be, and were—and after official persecution ended, there were hundreds of serious vigilante assaults on them throughout Britain, right through to the end of the nineteenth century. In reality, however, fairy scapegoats did produce a great deal of human suffering. The problem, here, was what people did to real human beings who were believed to be fairy changelings.

In August 1909, an old woman of Donegal, Annie McIntire, applied for a pension. She told the Pension Committee that although "she did not know the number of her years," she "remembered being stolen by the 'wee people' (fairies) on Halloween Night, 1839." Was she certain of this?

"Yes, by good luck, my brother happened to be coming home from Carndonagh that night, and I heard the fairies singing and saw them dancing around me in the woods at Carrowkeel. He had a book with him, and he threw it in among them. They then ran away." The applicant added that the people celebrated the event by feasting and drinking. The committee decided to grant her a pension.

Whatever happened that Halloween night, McIntire believed her version until the end of her days. So, too, would many of those around her, young or old. Everyone knew that fairies stole children.

More broadly, fairies again resembled vampires or witches in that all three, very basically, attacked life. The latter pair could suck out your blood, soul, or breath or extract the essence from food. Much later, that iconic Other of our times, the alien abductor, updated this basic assault with clinical probings or the removal of human eggs or sperm. In the pre-scientific cultures of the fairy or the witch, however, the most potent emblem of life was simply one's baby or child. One ironic result of this was that, for most of history, no child was delighted by fairies. Old people in Cornwall told Evans-Wentz: If we as children did anything wrong, the old folks would say to us, "The piskies will carry you away if you do that again.". . . In Tintagel, I used to sit around the fire at night and hear old women tell so much about piskies and ghosts that I was then afraid to go out of doors after darkness had fallen.

At Cwm Castell Fach farm in Wales, a seventy-year-old man told Evans-Wentz that "in his childhood days, a great dread of the fairies occupied the heart of every child. They were considered to be evil spirits who visited our world at night." Even in the less typically fairy-haunted flats of Norfolk, young children growing up around the First World War were told, "If naughty... that the 'hightie sprite' was at the bottom of the garden and would get them." On the whole, this distinctive East Anglian spirit evoked far less terror than Celtic fairies. There again, one 1980s informant recalled it as "a black bat-like figure, man-size, hovering silently in the twilight, waiting to snatch away disobedient children." While many boys and girls were being enchanted by Rose Fyleman's "fairies at the bottom of our garden," others still feared vampiric kidnappers at the bottom of theirs.

Writing in 1960, the Dutch scholar Jacoba Hooykaas found that child-stealing fairy or elf types were feared in Britain, Germany, France, the Netherlands, Moravia, Greece, Lithuania, Bohemia and Hungary, with a modern-day variant in Bali. In Celtic territories, fairies stole babies and children—especially boys, and especially those with blue eyes and fair hair—leaving fairy substitutes in their place. Having identified such a switch, people did everything they could to make the fairies reverse it. To the end of the nineteenth century, and probably later, such children were ritually abused by their parents to this end. Immersed in rivers or placed at the margin of coastal tides, stood on hot coals or hung over fires, exposed in freezing weather, bathed in poisonous foxglove essence, beaten, threatened, and subjected to forms of exorcism, these babies and children sometimes survived, sometimes not. Ironically, part of the logic of this treatment was the sense that the fairies cared enough about their offspring to rescue them from such abuses and restore their child in the process. Even as they tormented these supposed changelings, parents were projecting their familial love onto Fairyland.

Certain of these conditions only manifested some time after birth. This, surely, was the smoking fairy gun: you had known your baby, and this, now, was not him. Let us imagine a large rural family in which an initially normal, healthy new baby presently begins to seem suspect. He cries almost incessantly, fails to grow, walk, or talk, has oddly wizened features, and is constantly hungry. At one very basic level, a child continually crying and demanding food and unable to work like its six- or seven-year-old peers is a liability in such circumstances. But these problems almost certainly took second place to the real and frightening belief that it was not yours and that your child had been stolen. Hard as it now is to credit, parents in such cases very probably felt just as distraught as the modern mothers and fathers making television appeals about their missing or abducted children.

While it was clear to educated Victorians that many children were disabled children, much more precise clinical parallels were detailed in 1988 by the interdisciplinary scholar Susan Schoon Eberly. The case given above would fit especially well with a genetic disorder affecting metabolism, phenylketonuria (PKU). This and other similar conditions predominate among male children of Irish and English descent. Even brief references from fairy believers give clues to these disorders, talking of children like "old men," perhaps suffering from progeria. Obvious physical deformities, such as the oversized heads of hydrocephalus, or "water on the brain," would be singled out; yet so too might the pretty, blue-eyed, snub-nosed, "elfin" children afflicted with Williams syndrome. Here, as in every magical culture the world over, it was never a good idea to stand out. Eberly also adds that certain of these conditions only manifested some time after birth. This, surely, was the smoking fairy gun: you had known your baby, and this, now, was not him. All of this painstaking detective work can, in one sense, be collapsed into three letters: "oaf," a word broadly cognate with "elf," once meant not a clumsy or stupid person, but, literally, a changeling.

Plain and axiomatic as the real medical causes now seem to us, the majority view, from the ancient Romans to the Edwardian Celts, was intensely superstitious. When Martin Luther recommended drowning a child, it was because the child's appearance showed it to have no soul. In the seventeenth century, even the most rational Christians used "changeling" as a loose synonym for the mentally disabled, with dramatist Elkanah Settle echoing Luther when he talked, in 1694, of "some coarse half-souled fairy changeling." The relatively enlightened physician and philosopher John Locke probably did not believe in fairies, yet he did speculate at great length on the souls of the mentally disabled and whether or not they should be classified as a different species.

With these kinds of attitudes lodged at the heart of Christian and proto-scientific elites in the early modern period, what could changelings expect from true fairy believers? In all households, there were routine precautions aimed at preventing child theft. A very common one involved putting fire tongs over a cradle because of the fairies' well-known antipathy to iron. As in McIntire's case, books also had power over them, and religious ones especially—hence the placing of a Bible or prayer book under a child's pillow. In Ireland into the 1930s, babies were not believed safe from fairies until they (the babies) had sneezed, so many infants had pepper thrust under their noses minutes after birth.

In Connemara, at the same time, people still dressed boys and girls alike in red flannel petticoats until the age of twelve, a disguise used to trick those fairies who liked to steal boys in particular. Such measures failed, and the changeling met with violence—this often being advised or performed by the local fairy doctor. In some cases, such rituals were used on actual sick children thought to be "fairy-struck"—though, as we will see, they too could be seen as in danger of abduction.

Carole Silver cites changelings killed by foxglove baths in Wales in 1857 and in Donegal in the 1870s and 1890s. Eberly tells of a Scottish case in Caerlaverock, where the ceaselessly yelling and ill-tempered baby was thrown onto hot coals. In 1952, the Australian-born classical scholar Gilbert Murray (1866–1957) recalled how, in Ireland, in my lifetime, a child, who was for some reason reputed to be a changeling, was beaten and burned with irons, the mother being locked out of the room while the invading fairy was exorcised, though unfortunately, the child died in the process.

This killing does not seem to have been prosecuted, and many of those who escaped public or legal notice must now have been lost to us. This was nearly the case after the tragic death of a nine-year-old boy, the son of Kilkenny labourer Patrick Kearns. Late at night in April 1856, a police patrol met the Kearnses, taking their son's body to an unused burial ground, and insisted on examining him. Thus, instead of an unknown secret burial, there came to light the tale of how the child, confined to bed for three weeks past, was judged to be suffering from a "fairy blast." Although he was not himself a changeling, it was said that he was "being gradually carried off by the fairies"; if he had died naturally, it may have been believed that they had taken him. Versions of this affair vary. But it seems that a man called Thomas Donovan, assisted by Patrick Murphy, attempted a ritual test, giving the boy water and getting him to cough. When the boy could not cough, he was dragged violently out of the house and around the yard, strangled and badly beaten. He died early the next morning from his injuries. Even as they tormented these supposed changelings, parents were projecting their familial love onto Fairyland.

Some accounts have Donovan as the "fairy doctor" making the initial diagnosis; others mention an unnamed "wise woman" as doing so. Although one report has Patrick Kearns trying to rescue his son from Donovan, the versions that claim the parents to have agreed with the procedure, even after the boy's death, match other known cases better. Interestingly, during the trial, the judge briefly mentioned delusions about fairies, emphasising that these could in no way absolve Donovan (Murphy having by now fled to America). Meanwhile, could see no motive for the crime and wrongly inferred that perhaps there had been some delusion about the boy being "possessed by the Devil." This already shows the gulf between educated and popular perceptions of fairies. Moreover, we also learn that the Kearnses resorted to the fairy rituals despite their son having previously been under the care of two licensed doctors—

one of whom confirmed after an autopsy that the boy, though killed by Donovan, would have died of a tumour and water on the brain within a week. Donovan was sentenced to a year's hard labour. A few years before, the parents of six-year-old Mary Anne Kelly, allegedly "in a dying state" for six months before September 1850, turned from the dispensary physician to a Roscrea "fairy doctress" named Bridget Peters. Peters seems at one point to have declared Mary Anne "fairy struck" and at another that the child was a fairy. She gave the girl verbena and foxgloves and ordered that she be exposed naked outdoors for three nights on a shovel. This was done, despite Mary Anne's cries being audible in the house. On the third night, she died.

Here again, the fairy ritual took on demonic overtones. One report claimed that a prayer had to be said over the girl "in the name of the devil," and several carried the headline "Witchcraft." In this instance, the mother, Mary Kelly, seems to have been unusually complicit (and was initially tried along with Peters). If uneducated, the Kellys were by no means desperately poor. A key witness in the trial was their servant, Mary Maher, who was sacked after refusing to put Mary Anne out on the shovel and who may have been the only reason the crime came to light. Mary Kelly seems ultimately to have been acquitted. Peters, described as "respectable-looking" and literate, was found guilty.

Cases such as these now seem so extraordinary as to be almost unreal to us. Eberly has argued convincingly that modern-day responses of parents to disabled children still sometimes mingle anger and guilt and that such emotions could well have fed into the violence directed at changelings. Silver has suggested that one benefit of the changeling belief was the way it shifted blame for the child's condition into a thoroughly separate, supernatural realm, beyond human control. With these points in mind, it bears emphasising that Mary Anne had from birth been blind, brain-damaged, and partially paralyzed. Having said all this, we need to grasp that such modern rationalisations were largely alien from the fairy cultures in which changelings suffered or died. Most parents really, unshakably believed that this was a dangerous, uncanny fairy creature and very possibly feared it too.

In some cases, this level of terror was also apparent in the "fairy child." In April 1840, James Mahony, a man living on the country estate of Charles Riall at Heywood, County Tipperary, was influenced by his neighbours into the belief that his son, John (aged six or seven), was a fairy. This was partly due to a curvature of the spine that had kept the boy in bed for two years and partly to his being a suspiciously "intellectual child."

On the night of Tuesday, 14 April, Mahony, with the connivance of neighbours, held the near-naked boy over a hot shovel, threatening to put him on it, and dragged him halfway to the water pump, proposing to drown him under it if he did not reveal the whereabouts of Mahony's true son. John seems to have become so terrified by this that he presently "told them that he was a fairy and that he would send back the real John Mahony the next evening if they gave him that night's lodging"—even going so far as to specify that the real John was in a farmer's house, wearing corduroys and a green cap. The next morning, John was found dead in his bed.

Although a doctor decided that this had resulted from the boy's spinal condition, this fatality looks as though it may have been caused by sheer terror. We have seen that voodoo death can occur in such cases in around one to three days, while vagal inhibition can kill in seconds or minutes when shock affects the vagus nerve, the autonomic nervous system, and ultimately the heart. We have to wonder, here, if John's parents ever doubted the child's terrified "confession." Did they remain convinced that they had killed a fairy?

Similarly, Westropp remembered from his boyhood, in 1869, "a very old woman, Kate Molony," from Maryport, County Clare, who, many years before, being anxious about her daughter's failing health, "went to a 'wise woman,' who assured her that the child was 'changed.' She spoke of this on her return, and unfortunately the patient was old enough to understand the fearful decision. The poor child turned over on the bed with a groan and was later found to be dead. " This sounds unmistakably like vagal inhibition. If so, the child must have died either because of her sheer terror of her fairy status (which she believed) or because of the ensuing tortures that she knew this diagnosis would bring.

Such dangers were not entirely confined to the uneducated inhabitants of the Celtic countryside. Writing around 1865 about the fairies of Cornwall, Robert Hunt had recently heard from a friend how "the other day... an Irishwoman... was brought before the magistrates in New York for causing the death of a child by making it stand on hot coals, to try if it were her own truly-begotten child, or a changeling." Meanwhile, Westropp's family—affluent landowners at Patrickswell, Limerick, since the sixteenth century—had a much closer brush with changeling superstitions than the one recalled above. For Westropp's "second sister, whose delicacy, when an infant, excitedly remarked, was, about 1842, taken out by a servant to be exposed on a shovel on the doorstep at Carnelly. The angry and hasty intervention of another servant saved the child, but the would-be 'exposure' was convinced" of the rightness of her attempt to "'get back the child' from the fairies."

This incident partly echoes the 1884 case of three-year-old Philip Dillon of Clonmel, severely burned after two neighbours put him to a changeling test in his mother's absence. In such contexts, "changelings" were at risk from others besides their parents, with these people possibly acting "for the good of the community." It is easy to forget, looking back from a thoroughly medicalized world, how profoundly extra-scientific these people's lives were. The disabilities and illnesses of these children perhaps seemed just as fundamentally wrong. Changeling beliefs therefore offered two important benefits. First, they allowed people to shift from being helpless victims to active combatants of the perceived problem. Second, and probably more importantly, they gave an otherwise. frighteningly arbitrary condition a meaning—a known and accepted place within a shared framework of explanation.

Immersed in rivers or placed at the margin of coastal tides, stood on hot coals or hung over fires, exposed in freezing weather, bathed in poisonous foxglove essence, beaten, threatened, and subjected to forms of exorcism, these babies and children sometimes survived, sometimes not.

Yet, if this helps us make some sense of the majority of popular changeling cases, it fails to shed any light on the abuse suffered by Walter Trevelyan of Penzance. On Monday, July 10, 1843, local magistrates and residents heard of how the upper-middle-class Trevelyans had routinely tortured Walter, now aged two years and nine months, for at least a year at their grand Georgian house, The Orchard. Servants and visitors testified that Walter had been kept without food or water for hours, had been left outside in a tree during winter, been made to lie face down on the gravel walk, kicked over a slope in his baby carriage by his father, and was tied upside down in a tree until he was black in the face. After the miseries of the day, Walter was put to bed on a mattress filled with corks, lest he should gain any comfort in the few exhausted hours of the night.

Some of this was specifically ordered by Mrs Trevelyan, and all of it seems to have been the sole responsibility of Walter's parents. Indeed, although the hearing was catalysed by local vicar Reverend Le Grice, all of the evidence was supplied by working-class servants or visitors, with gardener Francis Dale stating that Walter's cries were so heartbreaking as to force him to move away to another part of the garden, where he could not hear them.

Was all this inspired by the belief that Walter had been "changed by the nurse"? Simon Young, to whom I am indebted for answering various queries on the original newspaper reports of the case, thinks not. He suspects that this phrase refers not to fairy changelings but to the belief that a child's nurse might change her affluent charge with her baby so that the latter could have the benefits of an elite upbringing. He adds that servants may have heard the parents remark facetiously that they thought the naughty Walter to have been "changed at nurse" (that is, so naughty that he could not be their natural child). They then took this literally as a partial explanation for the cruelties inflicted on him.

For educated parents to act on fairy beliefs in this way would be very unusual. We can further add that not all of the abuse looks precisely ritual—as, for example, John Trevelyan kicking Walter over the slope. But much of it, though different from popular habits in detail, does seem to fit the same broad logic: treat the child so badly that its fairy parents will reverse the switch. Ultimately, this case seems to me too unclear to permit a decisive judgment on its origins. One reason for this is that the Trevelyans themselves seem to have given no evidence at the hearing. Therefore, they have remained silent on why Walter was treated in this way. The final verdict grimly reinforces the impression that local magistrates essentially connived to spare the powerful family. The verdict clearly states that the child has been most cruelly and shamefully treated, but there isn't sufficient evidence to connect Mr Trevelyan with the ill-usage, preventing the case from being sent to a higher tribunal.

Hypothetically accepting that the parents' cruelty was purely mundane, we are faced with some curious ironies. Was it worse for people like the Trevelyans to torture their children than for fairy believers to do so, actuated by supernatural terrors? Yes. Second, we react to the household servants. It remains unclear whether they comprehended Walter as a human changeling or a fairy one. Given the popular fairy beliefs then prevalent in Cornwall, the latter notion would be plausible. The assumption here. Is the extreme cruelty of upper-middle-class parents so disturbing that it convinces others of its supernatural nature?

While we can imagine that Walter faced challenges in his adult life (even though they may have been less difficult than his childhood, such as his service in the Afghan War), it is unlikely that people treated him with suspicion and referred to him as a "changeling" whenever he passed by. Whatever Walter suffered in adult life (and fighting in the Afghan War, as he later did, was a walk in the park by comparison with childhood), we can assume that he did not find people around him looking askance and muttering "changeling" whenever he passed by. But this was the fate of a handful of adults who were mentally or physically disabled—people who were held by their neighbours, even parents, to be "fairies" throughout their lives. John Rhys heard in the late nineteenth century of a woman called Nani Fach at Llanover, Wales, supposed to be one of the fairies' offspring.

A study of the folklore records reveals that a range of objects, many of them extremely ordinary, are efficacious as charms that ward off or repel fairy harm. They fall into several broad categories, although most of them are natural materials.

Minerals
Several commonly occurring rocks and such substances seem to dispel the fairy's presence. Iron is by far the most famous of these, being effective in any shape—whether a knife, a horseshoe, a pin or needle, pairs of tongs, or the bolt of a door—but other less well-known (yet equally potent materials include:

A hot coal thrown in a vat of brewing ale will prevent the fairies from spoiling it. Likewise, live (that is, burning) coals carried by travellers will prevent them from being misled or abducted during their journey;
Amber beads sewn into a child's clothes will prevent its abduction.
Salt will certainly drive off the fairies, scattered around or put into foodstuff that you don't want to be stolen (I've discussed the power of salt separately);
In the Highlands, calves' ears were smeared with tar just before May Day to protect them against theft.

The last, rather well-known, natural object in this category is the so-called adder stone, a naturally holed stone that could be worn around the neck to protect an individual or might be hung over a byre or stable to safeguard the livestock. When not in use, the stones were often kept safe in iron boxes, which stopped the fairies from trying to interfere with them. The antiquarian Edward Lhuyd, visiting Scotland in 1699, recorded that these self-bored stones were also known as snake buttons, cock-knee stones, toad stones, snail stones, and mole stones.

'Elder at Walberswick' by Charles Rennie Mackintosh, 1915
Plants
It is pretty well known that sprigs of rowan repel faeries; other plants equally repulsive to the faeries are:

Fresh nettles, which, if laid on a milk churn, will stop them from hindering the churning (according to Manx belief). In this connection, see Guilpin's play Dialetheia (1598), in which a character says, "I applaud myself for nettle stinging thus this faery else."
Vervain and dill can dispel evil influences, as can milkwort and mugwort. Other handy herbs are mistletoe, nightshade, yarrow, groundsel, rue, and the sap of ash trees. Burnt bindweed would safeguard a baby in a crib, as would four leaves of clover.
In Wales, meanwhile, it was said that a four-leaf clover (combined, apparently, with nine grains of wheat) helped you

to see the fairies, which would certainly enable you to avoid them if need be.

On the Hebrides, St. John's Wort and pearlwort both granted general protection to cattle and people;

Sugar water, especially if it was served from a silver spoon or cup (or at least from a receptacle containing a silver coin), would help ensure that a mother and her newborn baby were safe from unwelcome family attention. Even humble tea drove fairies away in one Welsh case.

On Skye, oat cakes were said to have a protective effect. Quite whether this derives from the oats themselves or from the fact that they have been processed by baking and very possibly salted is less certain.

In County Durham, an elder branch was said to guard against witches and fairies. On the Isle of Man, the fairies were said to dwell in elder trees, but elder springs could also be carried to ward off the fairies—and even to strike them.

Also on Man, a willow cross would protect against buggies and fynoderees, but how much efficacy is derived from the wood and how much from the religious significance of the shape, I can't tell (see later for religious items).

The Crosh Bollan & Thor's Hammer
Animal Products

I've described the effects of stale urine before, but an odd variety of animal parts and by-products could prove revolting to fairies—some understandable, some more surprising:

Drawing blood was believed to drive off the fairies on Orkney and Shetland.

On the Isle of Man, two special animal bones were found to have powerful effects. These were the crash pollen, which is the upper part of the palate of the wrasse fish, and the so-called Thor's Hammer, which is in fact from a sheep's mouth and prevents fairy-leading. Manx fishermen would carry the crossbowman for protection at sea.

Burning leather repelled fairies from houses (see next section), as did the presence of a black cockerel.

Near Stirling, in central Scotland, it was recorded in 1795 that newborn calves would be forced to eat a little dung, as this would prevent both witches and elves from harming or stealing them.

Cloth Items

It's quite well known that red threads are effective against fairies, for example, tied around a child's throat to protect them from taking or woven into the hair of a cow's tail to prevent the fairies from stealing its milk. If you wanted to double your protection, securing a spring of rowan to someone or something with a red thread was recommended.

A burning rag carried around a woman in childbirth three times would stop the fairies from taking her and her newborn baby, it was said on Orkney and Shetland. It's also reported that, when the trows smelt the smoke from the rag, they would express their displeasure in a rhyme: "Wig wag, jig jag,/ Ill health so well/ That was stained/ Wi' a linen rag." To be fair, though, the smell of the smouldering material was probably the most effective part of this ceremony. For comparison, burning peats were also carried around farms on Shetland at Yule to ward off the trows. The combination of the smoke plus the flame (recall the lit coals earlier) appears to have been what discouraged the trows.

Wells & Well Water

As I have described previously, every kind has an ambivalent relationship to wells, sometimes inhabiting them, sometimes avoiding them, and sometimes giving their waters healing properties. In Wales, wells would be protected from the fairies by circling them with stones painted white; however, the water from some springs was reputed to keep the fairies at bay—for example, St Leonards Well at Sheep's Tor on Dartmoor.

Religious items

Linked to the possibly erroneous belief that fairies are fallen angels or emissaries of the devil and, as such, innately antithetical to all aspects of the Christian religion, items such as Bibles, psalms, and prayer books were constantly regarded as sure remedies against fairy threats. Even a few pages torn from a holy book could work, it was said in Scotland. It was found that an open Bible could be especially potent if carried around the person or place to be blessed and protected. On Shetland, plaiting crosses out of straws or the livestock's tail hairs was a further precaution undertaken.

As will be seen, a variety of items carried with you can provide excellent protection against fairy interference and abduction. Properly equipped, you should not need to fear being pixie-led or being taken. Luckily, too, although some of these items are quite rare, many are readily available to all.

The Faery Faith in Celtic Countries._Countries].

Evanze Wenze. Public Domain.

According to the testimony of anthropology, exorcism as a religious practice has always flourished wherever animistic beliefs have furnished it with the necessary environment, and not only has exorcism been a fundamental part of religious practices in past ages, but it is so at the present day. Among Christians, Celtic and non-Celtic, among followers of all the great historical religions, and especially among East Indians, Chinese, American first people men, Polynesians, and most Africans, the expelling of demons from men and women, from animals, from inanimate objects, and places is sanctioned by well-established rituals.

Exorcism as applied to the human race is thus defined in the *Dictionnaire de Theologie* (Roman Catholic) by L'Abbe Bergier: "Exorcism: conjuration, prayer to God, and command given to the demon to depart from the body of persons possessed.' The same authority thus logically defends its practice by the Church:

Far from condemning the opinion of the Jews, who attributed to the demon certain maladies, that divine master confirmed it.' Whenever exorcism of this character has been or is now generally practised, the professional exorcist appears as a personage just as necessary to society as the modern doctor, since nearly all diseases were and to some extent are still, both among Christians and non-Christians, very often thought to be the result of demon possession.

When we come to the dawn of the Christian period in Ireland and Scotland, we see Patrick and Columba, the first and greatest of the Gaelic missionaries, very extensively practising exorcism, and there is every reason to believe (though the data available on this point are somewhat unsatisfactory) that their wide practice of exorcism was quite as much a Christian adaptation of pre-Christian Celtic exorcism, such as the Druids practised, as it was a continuation of New Testament tradition. We may now present certain of the data that tend to verify this supposition, and using them, we shall be led to realise how fundamentally such an animistic practice as exorcism must have shaped the fairy faith of the Celts, both before and after the coming of Christianity.

'Once upon a time,' so the tale runs about Patrick, 'his foster mother went to milk the cow. He also went with her to drink a draft of new milk. Then the cow goes mad in the byre and kills five other kine: a demon, namely, enters her. There was great sadness in his foster mother, and she told him to bring the kine back to life.

Then he brought the kine to life so that they were whole, and he cured the mad one. So God's name and Patrick's were magnified thereby. " On another occasion, when demons came to Ireland in the form of blackbirds, quite after the manner of the Irish belief that fairies assume the form of crows, the Celtic ire of Patrick was so aroused in trying to exorcise them out of the country that he threw his bell at them with such violence that it was cracked, and then he wept: Now, at the end of those forty days and forty nights [of Patrick's long fast on the summit of Cruachan Aigle or Croagh Patrick, Ireland's Holy Mountain], 'the mountain was filled with blackbirds so that he knew not heaven or earth. He sang maledictive psalms at them. They left him not because of this. Then his anger grew against them. He strikes his bell at them so that the men of Ireland hear its voice, and he flung it at them, so that a gap broke out of it, and that [bell] is "Brigit's Gapling.".

Then Patrick weeps till his face and his chasuble in front of him are wet. No demon came to the land of Erin after that till the end of seven years and seven months and seven days and seven nights. Then the angel went to console Patrick and cleansed the chasuble and brought white birds Round Rock, and they used to sing sweet melodies for him.' In Adamnan's *Life of St. Columba,* it is said that 'according to custom', which in all probability was established in pagan times by the Druids and then maintained by their Christian descendants, it was usual to exercise even a milk vessel before milking and the milk in it afterwards.

Thus Adamnan tells us that one day a youth, Columban by name, when he had finished milking, went to the door of St. Columba's cell carrying the pail full of new milk that, *according to custom,* the saint might exorcise it. When the holy man had made the sign of the cross in the air, the air 'was greatly agitated, and the bar of the lid, driven through its two holes, was shot away to some distance; the lid fell to the ground, and most of the milk was spilled on the soil.'

Then the saint chided the youth, saying, Thou has done carelessly in thy work today; for thou hast not cast out the demon that was lurking in the bottom of the empty pail, by tracing on it, before pouring in the milk, the sign of the Lord's cross; and now not enduring, thou seest, the virtue of the sign, he has quickly fled away in terror, while at the same time, the whole of the vessel has been violently shaken and the milk spilt. Bring the pail nearer to me, that I may bless it.' When the half-empty pail was blessed, at the same moment it was refilled with milk. At another time, the saint, to destroy the practice of sorcery, commanded Silnan, a peasant sorcerer, to draw a vessel full of milk. from a bull, and by his diabolical art, Silvan drew the milk. Then Columba took it and said, 'Now it shall be proved that this, which is supposed to be true milk, is not so, but is blood deprived of its colour by the fraud of demons to deceive men; and straightway the milky colour was turned into its proper quality, that is, into blood.' And it is added that 'The bull also, which for the space of one hour was at death's door, wasting and worn by a horrible emaciation, in being sprinkled with water blessed by the Saint, was cured with wonderful rapidity.'

And today, as in the times of Patrick and Columba, exorcism is practised in Ireland and the Western Hebrides of Scotland by the clergy of the Roman Church against fairies, demons, or evil spirits when a person is possessed by them—that is to say, 'fairy-struck,' or when they have entered into some house or place; and on the Scottish mainland, individual Protestants have been known to practise it. A haunted house at Belachan, Perthshire, in which certain members of the Psychical Research Society had taken up summer quarters to 'investigate', was exorcised by the late Archbishop of Edinburgh, assisted by a priest from the Outer Isles.

Among the nine orders of the Irish ecclesiastical organisation of Patrick's time, one was composed of exorcists. The official ceremony for the ordination of an exorcist in the Latin Church was established by the Fourth Council of Carthage and is indicated in nearly all the ancient rituals. It consists of the bishop giving to the candidate the book of exorcisms and saying as he does so: 'Receive and understand this book, and have the power of laying hands upon demoniacs, whether they be baptised, or whether they be catechumens.' By a decree of the Church Council of Orange, making men possessed of a demon ineligible to enter the priesthood, it would seem that the number of demoniacs must have been very great. As to the efficacy of exorcisms, the Church Fathers during the first four centuries, when the Platonic philosophy was most influential in Christianity, agreed.

In estimating the shaping influences, designated by us as fundamental, which undoubtedly were exerted upon the Fairy Faith through the practice of exorcism, it is necessary to realise that this animistic practice holds a very important position in the Christian religion, which for centuries the Celtic peoples have professed.

One of the two chief sacraments of Christianity, that of baptism, is preceded by a recognised exorcism, as shown in the Roman Ritual, where we can best study it. In the exhortation preceding the rite, the infant is called a slave of the demon, and by baptism is to be set free. The salt that is placed in the mouth of the infant by the priest during the ceremony has first been exorcised by special rites. Then there follows before the entrance to the baptismal font a regular exorcism pronounced over the child: the priest taking some of his saliva on the thumb of his right hand, touches the child's ears and nostrils and commands the demon to depart out of the child. After this part of the ceremony is finished, the priest puts on the child's forehead a sign of the cross with holy oil. Finally, in due order, comes the actual baptism. And even after baptismal rites have expelled all possessing demons, precautions are necessary against a repossession: St. Augustine has said that exorcisms of precaution ought to be performed over every Christian daily, and it appears that faithful Roman Catholics who each day employ holy water in making the sign of the cross, and all Protestants who pray 'lead us not into temptation, but deliver us from evil', are employing such exorcisms: St. Gregory of Nazianzus writes, 'Arm yourself with the sign of the cross. which the demons fear and before which they take their flight,' and by the same sign, said St. Athanasius, 'All the illusions of the demon are dissipated and all his snares destroyed.' An eminent Catholic theologian asserts that saints who, since the time of Jesus Christ, have been endowed with the power of working miracles have always made use of the sign of the cross in driving out demons, curing maladies, and raising the dead. In the *Instruction sur le Rituel,* it is said that water that has been blessed is particularly designed to be used against demons; in the *Apostolic Constitutions,* formulated near the end of the fourth century, holy water is designated as a means of purification from sin and of putting the demon to flight. And nowadays, when the priest passes through his congregation casting over them holy water, it is an exorcism of precaution; or when, as in France, each mourner at a grave casts holy water over the corpse, it is undoubtedly—whether done consciously as such or not—to protect the soul of the deceased from demons who are held to have as great power over the dead as over the living.

Other forms of exorcism, too, are employed. For example, in the *Lebar Bible,* it is said of the Holy Scripture that by it the snares of devils and vices are expelled from every faithful one in the Church." From all this direct testimony, it seems to be clear that many of the chief practices of Christians are exorcisms, so that, like the religion of Zoroaster, the religion founded by Jesus has come to rest, at least in part, upon the basic recognition of eternal warfare between good and bad spirits for the control of man.

The curing of diseases through Christian exorcism is by no means rare now, and it was common a few centuries ago. Thus in the eighteenth century, beginning with 1752 and till his death, Gassner, a Roman priest of Closterle, diocese of Coire, Switzerland, devoted his life to curing people of possessions, declaring that one-third of all maladies are so caused, and fixed his headquarters at Ellwangen and later at Ratisbon. His fame spread over many countries in Europe, and he is said to have made ten thousand cures solely by exorcism. Not only are human ills overcome by exorcism, but also the maladies of beasts: at Carnac, on September 13, there continues to be celebrated an annual fete in honour of St. Comely, the patron saint of the country and the saint who (as his name seems to suggest) presides over domestic *horned* animals; and if there is a cow or even a sheep suffering from some ailment that will not yield to medicine, its owner leads it to the church door beneath the saint's statue, and the priest blesses it, and, as he does so, casts over it the exorcising holy water. The Church Ritual designates two forms of Benediction for such animals, one for those who are ordinarily diseased and another for those suffering from some contagious malady. In each ceremony, there comes first the sprinkling of the animal with holy water as it stands before the priest at the church door, and then there follows in Latin a direct invocation to God to bless the animal, 'to extinguish in it all diabolical powers,' to defend its life, and to restore it to health.

In 1868, according to Dr Evans, an old cow house in North Wales was torn down, and in its walls was found a tin box containing an exorcist's formula. The box and its enclosed manuscript had been hidden there some years previously to ward off all evil spirits and witchcraft, for evidently the cattle had been dying of some strange malady which no doctors could cure. Because of its unique nature and as an illustration of what Welsh exorcisms must have been like, we quote the contents of the manuscripts both as to spelling and punctuation as checked by Sir John Rhys with the original, except the undecipherable symbols that come after the archangels' names:

Lignum sanctae crisis defendant me a malis praesentibus preateritus & futuris; interioribus & exterioribus Daniel Evans Omnes spiritus laudet Dominum: Mosen habent & prophetas. Exergat Deus & disfeature inimitiesus—O Lord Jesus Christ, I beseech thee to preserve me, Daniel Evans, and all that I possess from the power of all evil men, women, spirits, wizards, or hardness of heart, and this I will trust thou will do by the same power as thou didst cause the blind to see the lame to walk, and they that were possessed with unclean spirits to be in their minds. Amen. Pater pater pater Noster Nostra Nostrum aia aia aia Jesus - Christus - Messyas - Emmanuel - Soter - Sabaoth - Elohim - on - Adonay - Tetragrammaton - Ag: - Pantheon - - Agios - Jasper - Melchor, - Balthasar Amen, etc. -- And by the power of our Lord Jesus Christ and His Heavenly Angels being our Redeemer and Saviour from all witchcraft and assaults of the Devil, Amen. O Lord Jesus Christ, I beseech thee to preserve me and all that I possess from the power of all evil men, women, spirits, or wizards past and present, or to come inward and outward. Amen.

From India, Mr. W. Crooke reports similar exorcisms and charms to cure and protect cattle. Thus there is employed in Northern India the 'the charm of the invincible protector,' one of 'Vishnu's titles, in his character as the earth-god Bhumiya—in Scotland, it would be the charm of the invincible fairy who presides over the flocks and to whom libations are poured—to exorcise diseased cattle or else to prevent cattle from becoming diseased.

This *Ajaypal jantra* is a rope of twisted straw, in which chips of wood are inserted. ' In the centre of the rope is suspended an earthen platter, inside which an incantation is inscribed with charcoal, and beside it is hung a bag containing seven kinds of grain.' The rope is stretched between two poles at the entrance of a village, and under it, the cattle pass to and fro from pasture. The following is the incantation found on one of the earthen saucers: Lord of the Earth, on which this cattlepen stands, protecting the cattle from death and disease! I know of none, save thee, who can deliver them.' In the Morbihan, Lower Brittany, we seem to see the same folk custom, somewhat changed to be sure; for on St. John's Day, the Christianised pagan sun festival in honour of the summer solstice, in which fairies and spirits play such prominent a part in all Celtic countries, just outside a country village a great fire is lit in the centre of the main road and covered over with green branches, to produce plenty of smoke, and then on either side of this fire and through the exorcising smoke are made to pass all the domestic animals in the district as a protection against disease and evil spirits, to secure their fruitful increase, and, in the case of cows, an abundant milk supply. Mr. Milne, while making excavations in the Carnac country, discovered the image of a small bronze cow, now in the Carnac Museum, and this would seem to indicate that before Christian times there was in the Morbihan a cult of cattle, preserved even until now, no doubt, in the Christian fete of St. Cornely, just as in St. Cornelius Fountain, there is preserved a pagan holy well.

It ought now to be clear that both pre-Christian and Christian exorcisms among Celts have shaped the fairy faith in a very fundamental manner. Anthropologically, the whole subject of exorcism falls in line with the psychological theory of the nature and origin of the belief in fairies in Celtic countries.

RECAP.

The cases dealt with in this and the succeeding chapters are, so far as the public knows, quite exceptional cases in Ireland. But the number of people more or less involved in two of them and the apparent acquiescence of entire localities in some or all of the proceedings raise them far above the category of ordinary crimes. These cases were hushed up and cloaked, or only partially reported, by the nationalist press of Ireland, and no public condemnation has been issued about them from either the pulpit, the press, or the platform—or the oracle at Maynooth. That is not right. There are thousands of "good, moral, industrious" peasants in country localities in Ireland who, if they do not firmly believe the superstitions that led to such horrible results in these cases, certainly border on those beliefs. If these dreadful cases are not indicative of any general condition of intense superstitious depravity in Ireland but are more or less isolated cases, then our note of condemnation should be all the more distinct and unequivocal. They are cases that occurred during the five years reviewed in this book and, therefore, come within its purview. Perhaps I attach more importance to them than they deserve. But, at all events, I have concluded that they afford food for reflection and that if they are to be narrated at all, they must be narrated in full. Let the reader skip this and the next chapter if he or she pleases; they do not affect the tenor of the book.

I sincerely pity all the people connected with these tragedies, but I pity still more intensely the many peasants who border upon if they do not firmly entertain, the beliefs expressed in these two cases. This latter feeling is the gadfly that urges me on, as it urges Socrates of old, to do what little I can to crush out those remnants of savagery, which should by this time be as extinct as the snakes in this so-called "Island of Saints."

The earliest knowledge we have of the Ballyvadlea case was what occurred on Wednesday, March 13, 1895. It was on Thursday the 14th that the brutal tragedy began, so far as the public will ever know, and it was consummated on the night of Friday the 15th and in the small hours of the morning of Saturday the 16th. Let the reader picture one of those new labourers' cottages, erected at the expense of the locality, and let by the guardians at a nominal rent, standing in its half-acre of ground close to the public road in the townland of Ballyvadlea, in the county of Tipperary. The district is far from the railway but is well-populated. It is in the parish of Drangan, and, I believe, in the Cashel archdiocese, and all the people connected with the tragedy are Catholics. Father Ryan, the curate, tells us that the Cleary's were "members of his congregation and under his spiritual charge," and that he knew them for four years and a half.

Michael Cleary, described to me as "a clever fellow" and by trade a cooper, and his wife, Bridget, were living in their new labourer's cottage, then, along with Mrs. Cleary's father, Patrick Boland. Mrs. Cleary, from all the accounts I can gather, was a handsome young woman, twenty-six years of age, who had been married for some years to Cleary and had had no children. In the words of Judge O'Brien, she was "a young married woman, suspecting no harm, guilty of no offence, virtuous and respectable in all her conduct and all her proceedings." Another witness says, "She was nice in manners and appearance." Cleary's own words, "She is too fine to be my wife," point to her physical beauty also. One who had frequently seen her before this dreadful business, on his way to hunt with the Tipperary hounds, tells me she was distinctly "good-looking." We have it that she wore gold earrings, and it leaks out accidentally that there is a canister with £20 in it in the house.

On Wednesday, then, which we shall call the first day, Dr. Crean called to see Mrs. Cleary at her house. He had been summoned on the 11th and "was not able to go till the 13th." He found her suffering from nervous excitement and a slight bronchitis. She was in bed, but the doctor "could see nothing in the case likely to cause death." Dr. Crean then gave her some medicine. He "had no anxiety about the case," left the house, and never saw her alive again. We, in the light of subsequent events, can well understand her "nervous excitement," although we are given no clue about anything that happened before this, the first day. She never uttered a word of complaint to the doctor, to the priest, or neighbour, or to a living person, about the agonies she was subjected to—tortures that equal some of the heinous doings of the Inquisition. Or, as the coroner, Mr J. J. Shee, J.P., to his lasting credit, put it at the inquest, "Amongst Hottentots, one would not expect to hear of such an occurrence."

The next actor on the scene is Father Ryan, who visited Mrs. Cleary on the same Wednesday afternoon. She was in bed. He says that "she did not converse with him, except as a priest, and her conversation was quite coherent and intelligible." He also left her on that day without, apparently, receiving any clue about the persecution and hellish misery of which she was the victim. If an unpierceable brass wall stood between this confessor and penitent, the confessor could not have been further away from the truth as to her condition. He, too, then walked out from that house on that spring afternoon, as ignorant of and as out of touch with her and those people of whom "he had spiritual charge," as if he were a marionette.

That is all we know about Wednesday, the 13th. The doctor saw her, thought her illness trivial, prescribed, and left. The curate heard her confession, gave her extreme function, and left out of touch with the poor sufferer, who had no friend on earth to whom she could open her inmost heart and thereby escape from the hideous doom which awaited her. There was no kindly human being in the locality to smell out this nest of horrors, no sharp, sympathetic eye to pierce beneath the surface and probe out her miseries.

We now come to Thursday, the second day. On the morning of Thursday, the 14th, Father Ryan says, "He was called to see Mrs. Cleary, but he told the messenger that having administered the last rites of the Church on the previous day, there was no need to see her again so soon! He did not consider her dangerously ill." The priest knew nothing at all, I hope and believe, about what was the matter with her. She, poor thing, was yearning for someone to speak to but could not get the words out. No need to see her again so soon! A professional ceremony then, it seems, had exhausted the whole duty of the clergyman; a professional ceremony in which, as is proved in this case, nothing vital, nothing essential, can have been revealed. The Rev. Father Ryan did not go to see her then, on the second day. How the morning and afternoon of this second day passed will never be known, but it is now our task to narrate the horrors of the evening. "It appears almost incredible," said Judge O'Brien afterwards at the trial, "that there could be such a degree of human delusion, that so many persons, young and old, men and women, could be so incapable of pity or sympathy with human suffering." He added that the crimes of that night "had spread a tale of horror and pity throughout the civilised world."

But if we are ignorant of the day's events, as we are of the events of the many previous days during which she must have been suffering persecution, our information as to the evening's and night's proceedings is explicit enough. William Simpson, a near neighbour of the Clearys, living only 200 yards off, accompanied by his wife, left their own house between nine and ten o'clock that evening to visit Mrs Cleary, having heard she was ill. When they arrived close to Cleary's house, they met Mrs Johanna Burke, accompanied by her little daughter, Katie Burke, and enquired from her how Mrs Cleary was. Mrs Burke, herself a first cousin of Mrs Cleary's, said, "They are giving her herbs, got from Ganey, over the mountain, and nobody will be let in for some time." These four people then remained outside the house for some time, waiting to be let in. Simpson heard cries inside and a voice shouting, "Take it, you b——, you old faggot, or we will burn you!" The shutters of the windows were closed and the door locked. After some time the door was opened and from within shouts were heard: "Away she go! Away she goes!" As Simpson afterwards learnt, the door had been opened to permit the fairies to leave the house, and the adjustment was addressed to those "supernatural" beings.

In the confusion, Simpson, his wife, Mrs. Burke, and her little daughter worked their way into the house. From this forward, we know some, at any rate, of the doings of the incarnate fiends and cowards assembled within these walls. Simpson saw four men—John Dunne, described as an old man, Patrick Kennedy, James Kennedy, and William Kennedy, all young men, "big, black-haired Tipperary peasants," as they were described to me by one who had to do with the case from start to finish, brothers of Mrs. Burke and first cousins of Mrs. Cleary, "holding Bridget Cleary down on the bed. She was on her back and had a nightdress on her. Her husband, Michael Cleary, was standing by the bedside."

Cleary called for a liquid and said, "Throw it on her." Mary Kennedy, an old woman, mother of Mrs. Burke, and all the other Kennedys present, brought the liquid. Michael Kennedy held the saucepan. The liquid was dashed over Bridget Cleary several times. Her father, Patrick Boland, was present.

William Ahearne, described as a delicate youth of sixteen, was holding a candle. Bridget Cleary was struggling, vainly, alas! on the bed, crying out, "Leave me alone." Simpson then saw her husband give her some liquid with a spoon; she was held down by force by the men for ten minutes afterwards, and one of the men kept his hand on her mouth. The men "at each side of the bed kept her body swinging about the whole time and shouting, 'Away with you! Come back, Bridget Boland, in the name of God!' She shouted horribly. They cried out, 'Come home, Bridget Boland.'

From these proceedings, Simpson gathered that "they thought Bridget Cleary was a witch" or had a witch in her, whom they "endeavoured to hunt out of the house by torturing her body."

Some time afterwards she was lifted out of the bed by the men, or rather demons, and carried to the kitchen fire by John Dunne, Patrick, William, and James Kennedy. Simpson saw red marks on her forehead, and someone present said they had to "use the red poker on her to make her take the medicine." The four men held poor Bridget Cleary in her nightdress over the fire, and Simpson "could see her body resting on the bars of the grate where the fire was burning." While this was being done, we learnt that the rosary was said. Her husband put some questions at the fire. He said if she did not answer her name three times, they would burn her. She, poor thing, repeated her name three times after her father and her husband!

"Are you Bridget Boland, wife of Michael Cleary, in the name of God?"

"I am Bridget Boland, daughter of Patrick Boland, in the name of God."

Simpson said they showed feverish anxiety to get her answers before noon.

"They were all speaking and saying, " Do you think it is her that is there? " And the answer would be 'Yes,' and they were all delighted."

After she had answered the questions, they put her back into bed, and "the women put a clean chemise on her," which Johanna Burke "aired for her." She was then asked to identify each person in the room and did so successfully. The Kennedys left the house at one o'clock "to attend the wake of Cleary's father," who was lying dead that night at Killenaule! Dunne and Ahearne left at two o'clock. It was six o'clock on the morning of the 15th, "about daybreak," when the Simpsons and Johanna Burke left the house after those hellish orgies. There had been thirteen people present in Cleary's house on that night, yet no one outside the circle of the perpetrators themselves seems to have known, or cared, if they knew, of the devilish goings-on in that labourer's cottage.

At one time during that horrible night, the poor victim said, "The police are at the window. Let ye mind me now! " But, alas, there were no police there!

We now come to the third day, Friday, 15th of March. Six

o'clock that morning found Michael Cleary, the chief actor, Patrick Boland, and Mary Kennedy in the house with the poor victim, when the two Simpsons and the two Burkes were leaving. Simpson says, "Cleary then went for the priest, as he wanted to have Mass said in the house to banish the evil spirits." This brings us back again to the Rev. Father Ryan, who says, "At seven o'clock on Friday morning I was next summoned. Michael Cleary asked me to come to his house and celebrate Mass; his wife had had a very bad night." Father Ryan, apparently as completely estranged from those members of his flock as if oceans rolled between, suspects nothing, sees nothing, knows nothing. Cleary "asked him to come to his house and celebrate Mass," for the celebration of which he was entitled to a fee, and he at once assented to that proposal. Father Ryan arrived at the cottage at a quarter past eight and said Mass in that awful front room where poor Bridget Cleary was lying in bed. He was the medium through which the miracle of transubstantiation was performed there and then, yet he had no glimmering of the atmosphere of hell in which he stood!

"She seemed more nervous and excited than on Wednesday," he says, and adds, "her husband and father were present before Mass began, but I could not say who was there during its celebration." He had no conversation with Michael Cleary "as to any incident which had occurred," because he suspected nothing. "When leaving," he said, "I asked Cleary, was he giving his wife the medicine the doctor ordered? Cleary answered that he had no faith in it. I told him that it should be administered. Cleary replied that people may have some remedy of their own that could do more good than doctors' medicine." Yet, Father Ryan left the house "suspecting nothing." "Did he have any suspicion of foul play or witchcraft?" He says, "he should have at once refused to say Mass in the house and have given information to the police." We have no personal censure for him. He too is a victim—the victim and the product of a system as rigid as iron, to discuss this would require a separate book.

After Father Ryan had said his Mass and left, she remained in bed. Simpson saw her there at midday and never saw her afterwards. His excuse for his presence and non-interference on Thursday night is that "the door was locked, and he could not get out." We find the names of still more people mentioned as having visited her that day. Thomas Smith, a farmer of Ballyvadlea, was ploughing in one of his fields, adjoining Cleary's house, on this day, and "hearing that she was ill, went in to see her." He only remained for ten minutes and went home. Other names are also mentioned as having been in the house that day—Meara, Tobin, Anglin, and Leahy, who called to see her also. Yet not to one of them did she utter a complaint, let us hope, about the persecution she was undergoing, nor do they seem to have noticed anything strange in what they must have seen and heard in that house. She seems, judging from the number of visitors, to have been extremely popular. Johanna Burke seems to have been in the house the greater part of this day. At one time she tells how Cleary came up to the bedside and handed his wife a canister and said there was £20 in it. She, a poor creature, took it, tied it up, "and told her husband to take care of it, that he would not know the difference till he was without it." She was "in her right mind, only frightened at everything." No wonder. Her brain must have been a particularly good one not to have become unhinged.

At length the night fell upon the scene, and, at eight o'clock Cleary, who seems to have ordered all the other actors about as if they were hypnotised, sent Johanna Burke and her little daughter Katie for "Thomas Smith and David Hogan." Smith says, "We all went to Cleary's and found Michael Cleary, Mary Kennedy, Johanna Meara, Pat Leahy, and Pat Boland in the bedroom." The husband had a bottle in his hand and said to the poor bewildered wife, "Will you take this now, as Tom Smith and David Hogan are here? In the name of the Father, Son, and Holy Ghost!" Tom Smith, a man who said "he had known her always since she was born," then enquired what was in the bottle, and Cleary told him it was holy water.

Poor Bridget Cleary said "yes," and she took it. She had to say, before taking it, "In the name of the Father, Son, and Holy Ghost," which she did. Smith and Hogan then left the bedside and "went and sat at the fire." Cleary told them that his wife, "as she had company, was going to get up." She left her bed, put on "a frock and shawl," and came to the kitchen fire. The talk turned upon pishogues, or witchcraft and charms. Smith remained there till noon and then left the house, leaving Michael Cleary (husband); Patrick Boland (father); Mary Kennedy (aunt); Patrick, James, and William Kennedy (cousins); Johanna Burke, and her little daughter Katie (also cousins), behind him in the house. Thomas Smith never saw Bridget Cleary after that. According to Johanna Burke, they continued "talking about fairies," and poor Bridget Cleary, sitting there by the fire in her frock and shawl, wan and terrified, had said to her husband, "Your mother used to go with the fairies; that is why you think I am going with them."

"Did my mother tell you that?" exclaimed Cleary.
"She did. That she gave two nights with them," replied she.

This shows us that Cleary had drunk in superstition with his mother's milk. Johanna Burke then says that she made tea and "offered Bridget Cleary a cup." But Cleary jumped up, and getting "three bits of bread and jam," said she would "have to eat them before she could take a sup." He asked her as he gave her each bit, "Are you Bridget Cleary, wife of Michael Cleary, in the name of the Father, Son, and Holy Ghost?" The poor, desolate young woman answered twice and swallowed two pieces. We all know how difficult it is when wasted by suffering and excited by fear, to swallow a bit of dry bread without a drop of liquid to soften it. It, in fact, was the task set to those in the olden days who had to undergo the "ordeal by bread." How many of them, we are told, failed to accomplish it? Poor Bridget Cleary failed now at the third bit presented to her by the demon who confronted her. She could not answer the third time.

He "forced her to eat the third bit." He threatened her, "If you won't take it, down you go!" He flung her to the ground, put his knee on her chest, and one hand on her throat, forcing the bit of bread and jam down her throat.

"Swallow it, swallow it. Is it down? Is it down?" he cried.

The woman, Burke, says she said to him, "Mike, let her alone; don't you see it is Bridget that is in it?" and explains, "He suspected it was a fairy and not his wife."
Let Burke now tell how the hellish murder was accomplished: "Michael Cleary stripped his wife's clothes off, except her chemise, and got a lighted stick out of the fire and held it near her mouth. My mother (Mary Kennedy), brothers (Patrick, James, and William Kennedy), and myself wanted to leave, but Cleary said he had the key of the door, and the door would not be opened till he got his wife back."

I wanted to leave! Cowards, dolts!" They were crying in the room and wanting to get out." This crowd in the room was crying while Cleary was killing their first cousin in the kitchen.

"I saw Cleary throw lamp oil on her. When she was burning, she turned to me" (imagine that face of woe!) "and called out, 'Oh, Han, Han!' I endeavoured to get out for the peelers. My brother William went up into the other room and fell in a weakness, and my mother threw Easter water over him. Bridget Cleary was all this time burning on the hearth, and the house was full of smoke and smell. I had to go up to the room; I could not stand it. Clearly then came up into the room where we were and took away a large sack bag. He said, 'Hold your tongue, Hannah; it is not Bridget I am burning. You will soon see her go up into the chimney.' My brothers, James and William, said, 'Burn her if you like, but give us the key and let us get out.' While she was burning, Cleary screamed out, 'She is burned now. God knows I didn't mean to do it.' When I looked down into the other room again, I saw the remains of Bridget Cleary lying on the floor on a sheet. She was lying on her face, and her legs turned upwards, as if they had contracted in burning. She was dead and burned."

Cleary next asked Patrick Kennedy to assist him in burying the body "until he could lay her beside her mother." According to his sister, Mrs. Burke, Patrick Kennedy at first refused. His account, when charged before the magistrates, was that he went with Cleary to bury her "for fear he would be killed." He had nothing to do, he said, with the actual burning on that night; he "heard a roar" from the room in which he was, that was all; adding, "I am cracked after it to see my first cousin burned." James Kennedy said, in court, that "on the second (Friday) night he asked Clearly for the love of God not to burn his wife, and he added that they had gone three nights to the Fort at Kylenagranagh but did not see anything.

As this is the first mention of the word "fort," let me say at once that it means a ring fence, or double ring fence, of simple earth, thrown up in ancient times by the Danes, or other settlers in Ireland, in the manner of a Zulu kraal. The South of Ireland is studded with them, and though they are often most inconveniently situated on tillage land, and though their destruction presents no features of difficulty whatever, beyond merely levelling the fence, they have been preserved, from a superstitious dread of ill luck to anyone who ventured to destroy them. I am informed that people in Ballyvadlea believe that a person being near this fort at night is liable to be struck with rheumatism, paralysis, and so forth! Those accursed, unlovely, and useless remains of barbarism should be levelled to the ground by every man who wishes to see Ireland prosper. I know a score of farmers who have these forts on their land: all farmers of the best class, comfortable, rational, hospitable, intelligent, keen men of business; yet, not one of them dares to remove these nuisances from their holdings, although they continually grumble at the inconvenience they cause.

Observe now the cool generalship displayed by Cleary. William Kennedy says that "when he came out of the room, he saw Bridget Cleary blazing; he asked Cleary what he was doing. Cleary said it was nothing to him. He asked to be let out. Cleary wouldn't let him."

No! But "Cleary himself then went out and locked the door after him" and left those four male and three female human beings in the house with the burned body. Out into the night with him, searching, no doubt, for a trusty, secret spot in which to put the body. The hiding place he selected was over a mile distant from the cottage! "When he came back, he got Pat Kennedy to go out with him," and they buried her! Yes, and so well selected was the spot where the body was not found for six days afterwards by the police.

Now, behold Cleary and Patrick Kennedy returning to the house, having gotten rid of their horrible burden after an absence of two hours. Johanna Burke says, "My mother, my two brothers, Pat Boland, my daughter, and myself were made prisoners till they came back." Cleary had locked the door on the outside! Cleary then, on his return, confronted Johanna Burke, and she says, "He told me to say that I went to prepare her a drink and, when returning, met her at the door, and that she spat at me and went out of the door, and that I could not say where she went to." That was the story to be concocted to explain her disappearance. Cleary said that "he would go down towards Cloneen and pretend he was half mad." Then he said to Johanna Burke, "Hannah, it is hard to depend on you; but if you were to be kept in jail till you rot, DON'T TELL."

Johanna Burke then says, "I went down on my knees and declared before God and man that, until the day I died, I would never tell, even if she was found." Cleary next faced his father-in-law, and, including Johanna Burke in his glance, said, "I dread the two of you." Old Boland said, "Now that my child is burned, there is no use in saying anything about it; but God help me in the latter end of my days!"

It was now daylight on Saturday morning, the 16th of March, the fourth day, and Johanna Burke "saw Michael Cleary washing the trousers of his light tweed suit that he had on him. There were stains like grease on it, and he exclaimed, 'Oh God, Hannah, there is the substance of poor Bridget's body!'" He also picks up one of his wife's earrings and destroys it, lest it should be evidence against him. John Dunne, who was not present at all on the Friday night, now reappears upon the scene. He is the man who is said to have suggested holding her over the fire on Thursday night, but, in mitigation, he says, "They did not burn her that night; they only held her over the fire!" On this Saturday morning, he came up to Cleary's house and "found her gone." Cleary, in explanation of her disappearance, told him the story that he had already concocted for Johanna Burke, adding that "he thought she was gone with the fairies." Dunne offered to search for her, and with Cleary accepting his offer, the two men set off for Kylenagranagh Fort and searched it and the whole neighbourhood near it.

Cleary said, "She used to be meeting an Eggman in the lower road about a mile and a half away." The peasant women, living in the by-roads, used to come out with their eggs to meet this eggman on the main road. As proof of Bridget Cleary's thrift, Cleary now insinuates to Dunne that he thought it possible that she had gone to meet the eggman!

Having searched everywhere in vain, Cleary could not keep up the self-restraint any longer, and he burst out, "She was burned last night!" Ignorant and deplorable a human being as Dunne may be, there is some spark of energy and manliness in his character, and I believe his story.

"You vagabond," said Dunne, "why did you do it?"
"She was not my wife," replied Cleary; "she was too fine to be my wife. She was two inches taller than my wife."

But Dunne brushed him aside and said, "Go now and give yourself up to the authorities and to the priest. You will have no living on earth."

Cleary replied, "Well, I will if you'll come along with me." Dunne consented, and they went towards Drangan. They met Michael Kennedy on the road, and he went back to Drangan with them. He had not been present at the Friday night's doings either. There are various versions of how the communication was made to the priests. Father Ryan says, "he saw Cleary kneeling near the altar, very nervous, and asked him into the vestry;" that Cleary "suggested going to confession, but I would not allow him, as I did not think him fit to do so! I coaxed him into the yard. I began to feel afraid of him." Not fit to do so! Is not repentance the only cure for the agony of the mind? Michael Kennedy took Cleary from the precincts of the chapel without confession.

John Dunne says he told the Rev. Father Ryan that "they had burned her to death last night and buried her; and that he had been asking Cleary all the morning to give her Christian burial." Christian burial; wait until you hear the sequel of the case! Father Ryan says, "He was horror-struck and could not remember what reply he made; his only thought was, How could three or four of them go out of their minds simultaneously?"

Suffice it to say, the priests only told the police that "they suspected there was foul play," and, with this vague direction, blindfolded Justice was started on the track.

John Dunne says he told the parish priest, whose name has not been allowed to appear in print in connection with the case and which I shall not mention either. Dunne says that as they walked home from Drangan, they saw a policeman following them. Justice, in the person of Acting-Sergeant Egan, met Cleary later on in the day "on the road near Cloneen," where Cleary said he would go "and pretend to be half mad," you remember. Acting Sergeant goes to Cleary's house with him, asking him questions about his wife. Cleary tells him "She left home about twelve o'clock last night" and mentions that "Johanna Burke had been at the house last night" and also that his father-in-law had slept in the next room. The two people whom Cleary had coached, you remember, in the morning. Not much madness here, only the pretence of madness, which he foretold in the morning he would assume. Pat Boland is also there, and in reply to a query, cries and says, "My daughter will come back to me." The restless acting sergeant goes off, but returns at ten o'clock at night and finds the house deserted and doors locked—like some hellish theatre after the tragedy had been performed! He gets himself in through the window and finds a burned nightdress. Where Cleary and Boland were, we do not know. Simpson does not appear to have seen Clearly at all on this day, Saturday.

Johanna Burke is taken in hand by the police and deposed: "I was at the house on the night of the 15th. Bridget Cleary was raving. After some time, she got up and dressed and sat at the fire. She afterwards went to bed. I went out for some sticks. When I returned, I met her at the doorway, going out in her nightdress. I endeavoured to hold her and failed. Since that night, I have not seen her. Her husband followed her for some time and returned. He did not see her. She has been missing ever since, and they searched for her." Simpson also deposes what he knows of Thursday night's doings before being quoted, and says "he heard she was missing since Friday night."

Now, blindfolded Justice, double-bandaged, what are you to do? You can arrest the five Kennedys, mother and sons, and John Dunne and William Ahearne and Cleary and old Boland, or watch them like a cat watching wicked rats, and keep Burke and your Simpson, your mainstays, close in hand. All of these things are well done. These rats, then under the surveillance of the cats of justice, are allowed to play for a day or two.

Sunday, the 17th of March, St. Patrick's Day, now dawns. Moore's words, associated with this national holiday, are inappropriate in Ballyvadlea today:

"Though dark are our sorrows, to-day we'll forget them, and shine through our tears like a sunbeam in showers; There never were hearts; if our rulers would let them, more formed to be grateful and blessed than ours."

Our rulers cannot well be blamed for this sad business in Ballyvadlea, our political rulers!

Simpson saw Cleary on this Sunday morning, and Cleary told him that "his wife left home at midnight on Friday." Between seven and eight that evening, Simpson saw him again, and Cleary asked him for a revolver, saying "that these parties who had convinced him about his wife would not go with him to the fort"—that execrable fort at Kylenagranagh Hill. "It appeared to me," says Simpson, "that they had convinced him that his wife had gone with the fairies. The fort was supposed to be a fairies' habitation. He said she would be riding on a grey horse. She told him so. And he said they should cut the ropes tying her on the saddle and that she would then stay with him if he was able to keep her." Simpson refused to give him the revolver. What a pity Simpson had not got his revolver with him on Thursday night! Simpson afterwards saw Cleary going to the fort with a big table knife in his hand to cut the ropes and set her free from the grey horse, presumably! Did he think of suicide, or was he still keeping up the pretence of madness?

During the interval that now elapses between the 17th and the 21st of March, the police are busily searching for the body, assisted by Michael Kennedy, who was not in the house on a Friday night. The police, thus set upon a false scent, under that able young man, District Inspector Wansbrough, who certainly deserves to rise high in the Royal Irish Constabulary, proceed to search and scour the entire countryside. Railway stations are watched; farmhouses and outhouses are searched; fields, woods, glens, and brakes are tried in all directions; ponds and rivers are dragged! Neither priests nor participants give any assistance to the police.

At length, when, after several days, no trace is discovered of this woman who had left her house at midnight, arrayed only in her nightdress, District Inspector Wansbrough rightly concludes that she must be dead. If Bridget Cleary's body was not discovered, no further effective proceedings could be taken. No crime, whatever could be laid the charge of those people. It seemed a hopeless quest that the police now entered upon. Hundreds of square miles of country to search for one poor half-burned body lying in a few square feet of earth! No assistance, no clue, though so many people around them knew everything!

All the parties—McCleary himself, Boland, Dunne, the five Kennedys, and William Ahearne—were arrested. The neighbourhood was abuzz with the mystery of the missing woman. On the 21st, the prisoners are brought before the magistrates in open court at Clonmel, with Simpson's depositions and Johanna Burke's false, Cleary-concocted story being the only basis on which the prosecution has to work. Denis Ganey, who is said to have supplied the herbs, is arrested but afterwards released. There was no case against him, whatever. His herbs were, perhaps, as good as much of the stuff called doctors' medicine. Nothing was elicited to elucidate the mystery. Cleary, Pat Boland, Pat Kennedy, and his mother and two brothers all kept their secret well. Old Boland goes so far as to say from the dock, "I have three more persons that can say she was strong the night she went away; she got up and dressed." This would go to prove, you see, that what they had done to her on Thursday night—which was all they were charged with so far—had inflicted no serious injury on her—was, in fact, a fatherly kind of curative treatment! Their cuteness is the most astonishing thing about this gang of people. Their appearance, under arrest, in the streets of Clonmel was greeted with "yells, hisses, and groans," but their demeanour in the dock is described as "unconcerned: they chatted and exchanged pinches of snuff with each other."

But, notwithstanding all their cunning, discovery was at hand. After the Court had adjourned and the prisoners were remanded to jail, District Inspector Wansbrough directed the police at Cloneen, Drangan, and Mullinahone "to make a deliberate search" once again for the body. It was the next day, Friday, 22nd March, that Sergeant Rogers, keen on the scent, when crossing some furzy ground, noticed "some broken thorn bushes freshly cut from a hedge in an angle of a field." And there, under a shallow covering of clay, only a few inches deep, the body of poor Bridget Cleary was discovered at a spot considerably over a mile from the cottage. It presented "a most terrible appearance," with the back and lower part all burned but the head preserved and "features perfect!" Marvellous preservation. There was no clothing on the body, except the stockings. Her head was enveloped in a sack, and in her left ear was one of her gold earrings. Her limbs were cramped up, and her arms were folded across her breast. Constable Somers, who knew her for three years, identified her "by her features—they were perfect." He had last seen her about a month or six weeks before.

I shall not give the gruesome description of the doctors who made the post-mortem, how the muscles of the spine were burned and the bones exposed, and so forth, and the deadly purple marks of strangulation, with others too horrible to mention. Suffice it to say, the burns were "the cause of death," which was all the coroner's jury wanted to know. The coroner's jury did not go into the attendant facts but found that the burns, inflicted by some persons unknown, caused the death of the young, handsome, thrifty Bridget Cleary. Had not the body been discovered, the world might never have heard of the Ballyvadlea case!

The inquest was held in a vacant house near where the body was found. After the conclusion of the proceedings, not a single human being, male or female, clerical or lay, would lend any assistance to give a Christian burial to the body. Horror of horrors! The police had to bury Bridget Cleary's corpse that night, by the light of a lantern, in Cloneen churchyard. We shall find the Maynooth theologians, in a later chapter, arguing that "the existence of motion proves the existence of a necessary being apart from the world." Fudge! I tell them that they will have to answer for this case and the Lisphelan case;

I hope and pray when they are confronted with that "necessary being."

About the police, let me say that it is because of their action in cases like this and the Lisphelan case, now about to be described, that I shall never be found saying a word against the Royal Irish Constabulary, no matter what views I may hold about the expensive character of its establishment. The policemen act like Christians, at any rate, and they stand between us and barbarism in such cases as this.

It was now, after the discovery of the body, on the second day of the magisterial investigation, that all the dreadful facts of Friday night's doings were divulged by Johanna Burke. The end draws near at last. The prisoners were returned for trial to the Clonmel Assizes in July by the presiding magistrates, Colonel Evanson, R.M., and Mr. Grubb, J.P., after a prolonged investigation, during which "the 'cuteness and coolness" of the accused were manifested more than once. Addressing the jury, Judge O'Brien, himself a Roman Catholic and not a nominal one either, said: "This case demonstrates a degree of darkness in the mind, not of one person but of several, a moral darkness, even religious darkness, the disclosure of which had come with surprise on many persons." One would hope so! But the leniency of the sentences also, it may be truly said, came as a surprise to many people. The charge of murder was withdrawn by the Crown prosecutor! Cleary was therefore found guilty, not of murder, but of manslaughter, and was sent to penal servitude for twenty years; Patrick Kennedy, found guilty of wounding, "the most guilty of all, except Michael Cleary," in Judge O'Brien's opinion, got five years' penal servitude; John Dunne, the least contemptible of them, got three years' penal servitude; William and James Kennedy, a year and a half's imprisonment each; Patrick Boland and Michael Kennedy, six months; and when Mary Kennedy's turn came, the Judge said tearfully, "I will not pass any sentence on this poor old woman."

Thus ends this tale of "moral darkness, even of religious darkness, not of one person, but of several," the events of which took place, not in Darkest Africa, but in Tipperary; not in the ninth or tenth, but at the close of the nineteenth century; not amongst Atheists, but amongst Roman Catholics, with the Rosary on their lips, and with the priest celebrating Mass and administering absolution and extreme unction in their houses.

Ah, my readers, Ireland is not the merry country that people think, which Protestant Irishmen like Lever and Lover have painted it; or the abode of half-humorous, half-contemptible braggarts, as Thackeray saw it. It is a sad, gloomy, depressed, and joyless country for the bulk of its peasantry. Hence, they leave it. When the heart is sad and the mind clouded in ignorance and oppressed by the darkest fears and mysteries, there can be no humour, no gaiety. There is, I have always believed, more real gaiety of heart in one cooker on the Old Kent Road than in all the Catholic peasants of Munster.

*"The wind blows east, the wind blows west,
And there comes good luck and bad;
The thriftiest man is the cheerfulest;
'Tis a thriftless thing to be sad, sad,
'Tis a thriftless thing to be sad." – Carlyle.*

The legends
A mother had her child taken from the crib by elves. In its place, they laid a changeling with a thick head and staring eyes who would do nothing but eat and drink. In distress, she went to a neighbour and asked for advice. The neighbour told her to carry the changeling into the kitchen, set it on the hearth, make a fire, and boil water in two eggshells. That should make the changeling laugh, and if he laughs, it will be all over with him. The woman did everything just as her neighbour said. When she placed the eggshells filled with water over the fire, the blockhead said:
Now I am as old
as the Westerwood,
but I have never seen anyone cooking in shells!
And he began laughing about it. When he laughed, a band of little elves suddenly appeared. They brought the rightful child, set it on the hearth, and took the changeling away. The following true story took place in the year 1580. Near Breslau, there lived a distinguished nobleman who had a large crop of hay every summer, which his subjects were required to harvest for him. One year there was a new mother among his

harvest workers, a woman who had barely had a week to recover from the birth of her child. When she saw that she could not refuse the nobleman's decree, she took her child with her, placed it on a small clump of grass, and left it alone while she helped with the haymaking. After she had worked a good while, she returned to her child to nurse it. She looked at it, screamed aloud, hit her hands together above her head, and cried out in despair that this was not her child. It sucked the milk from her so greedily and howled in such an inhuman manner that it was nothing like the child she knew.

As is usual in such cases, she kept the child for several days, but it was so ill-behaved that the good woman nearly collapsed. She told her story to the nobleman. He said to her, "Woman, if you think that this is not your child, then do this one thing. Take it out to the meadow where you left your previous child and beat it hard with a switch. Then you will witness a miracle."

The woman followed the nobleman's advice. She went out and beat the child with a switch until it screamed. Then the Devil brought back her stolen child, saying, "There, you have it!" And with that, he took his child away.

This story is often told and is known by both the young and the old in and around Breslau.

A living superstition
We all want explanations for happenings that fall outside of our control, especially those that have a direct bearing on our

welfare. It is only natural that our forebears wanted to know why some children fail to develop normally and what our responsibilities are towards these handicapped individuals. The two stories quoted above are part of a vast network of legends and superstitions that give primitive but satisfying answers to these questions. These accounts, which, unlike most fantasy tales, were widely believed, suggest that a physically or mentally abnormal child is very likely not the human parents' offspring at all, but rather a changeling—a creature begotten by some supernatural being and then secretly exchanged for the rightful child. {footnote 3} From pre-Christian until recent times, many people have sincerely and actively believed that supernatural beings can and do exchange their inferior offspring for human children, making such trades either to breed new strength and vitality into their diminutive races or simply to plague humankind.

These beliefs continued to exert influence well into the nineteenth century, and in some areas even later. Writing In England in 1890, the pioneering folklorist Edwin Sidney Hartland stated: "In dealing with these stories [about changelings], we must always remember that not merely are we concerned with sagas of something long past, but with a yet living superstition." In 1911, W. Y. Evans-Wentz, himself a true believer in the reality of fairy life, published an extensive study,

The Fairy Faith in Celtic Countries contains numerous accounts of exchanged children. This book, with a new introduction praising the author for his courageous acceptance of "a greater reality beyond the everyday world," was reissued in 1966. As late as 1924, it was reported that in sections of rural Germany, many people were still taking traditional precautions against the demonic exchange of infants. Finally, writing in 1980, Hasan M. El-Shamy reports: "The belief that the jinn may steal a human infant and put their infant in its place is widespread in numerous parts of Egypt." {footnote 6} Views held firmly for a thousand years do not die easily, especially when they appear to answer some of life's most troublesome questions.

The legend genre

In keeping with their higher level of popular credibility, changing accounts are much more often classified as legends than as fairy tales by folktale scholars. The Grimms themselves delineate between these two principal folktale genres in terms that twentieth-century folklorists still find meaningful: "The fairy tale is more poetic, the legend is more historical... While it is the children alone who believe in the reality of fairy tales, the folk have not yet stopped believing in their legends." {footnote 7} Legends, they conclude, are less fantastic and more firmly rooted in reality than fairy tales. Storytellers use a variety of literary devices to emphasise the familiarity and credibility of their changing accounts. In contrast to fairy tales, which nearly always take place at an indefinite "once upon a time" and in an unnamed place, changing legends frequently are set in a precisely identified time and location. The opening of "Beating the Changeling with Switches" is typical in this regard: "The following true story took place in 1580. Near Breslau, there lived a well-known nobleman. " Another changeling tale begins with the sentence, "A reliable citizen of Leipzig told the following story.

Martin Luther on changelings
The Grimms do not identify their "reliable citizen of Leipzig," but they do identify another of their sources, a man whose name certainly carried a great deal of authority and respect throughout Protestant Germany: Martin Luther. The influential church reformer was not only an avid storyteller, but, as his writings demonstrate, he was also a true believer in changelings. Luther was very much a product of his times concerning superstitious beliefs and practices. He sincerely believed that Satan was responsible for the malformed children known as changelings and that such satanic child exchanges occurred frequently. {footnote 9} In Luther's theological view, a changeling was a child of the devil without a human soul, "only a piece of flesh." This view made it easy to justify almost any abuse of an unfortunate child thought to be a changeling, including the ultimate mistreatment: infanticide. Luther himself had no reservations about putting such children to death. Shared responsibility

Despite the general credibility given to changing accounts and the support that they received from respected church leaders (Catholics as well as Protestants), there is evidence that many people were uneasy about the cruel treatment that the legends seemed to advocate. This evidence comes from the stories themselves. Parents who suspect that their child has been replaced with a changeling rarely decide on a course of action without first receiving advice and moral support from a third party. This fact is stated or implied in virtually all changeling tales, although it is usually communicated in an offhand manner.

For example: "In distress, she [the mother] went to her neighbour and asked her for advice." The parents of seriously handicapped children wanted others to share the moral responsibility for whatever decisions were reached. Folklore suggests that parents sought and received advice and approval from all segments of society before taking any drastic measures with their suspected children. The Grimms' accounts offer excellent examples of this broadly based community support: In three of their tales, the advice comes from ordinary people: a neighbour, a stranger on the street, and an unidentified person. In two other instances, the mothers—peasant women—are advised by their feudal landlords, and in one tale, "The Changeling in the Thuringian Forest," {footnote 12} the mother receives information from her pastor that enables her to discover her changeling's true identity and to drive him away. Several levels of community support are suggested by the sources of advice in these changing stories. Peer approval is indicated by the participation of ordinary people in the parents' decisions, and the voice of civil and ecclesiastical authority is added by the pronouncements of the landlords and the clergy.

Justifying infanticide

The cruelty to which suspected changelings are subjected in folktales makes it clear why the perpetrators of this harsh treatment sought the symbolic approval of their community. In the Grimms' accounts alone, we learn of changelings being thrown into the water, beaten severely with a switch, left unfed and crying in an open field, or placed on a hot stove. This list of ordeals can easily be expanded by consulting other changeling tales from throughout northern Europe. There is ample evidence that these legendary accounts do not misrepresent or exaggerate the actual abuse of suspected changelings. Court records between about 1850 and 1900 in Germany, Scandinavia, Great Britain, and Ireland reveal numerous proceedings against defendants accused of torturing and murdering suspected changelings. Similar incidents were undoubtedly even more common in earlier centuries, but before the mid-19th century, public opinion, religious attitudes, and legal indifference made it unlikely that such cases would be prosecuted. The court records of Gotland, Sweden, for 1690 documents one of the rare exceptions. A man and woman were placed on trial for having left a ten-year-old "changeling"—a sickly child who was not growing properly—on a manure pile overnight on Christmas Eve, hoping that the elves who had made the exchange some years earlier would now return their rightful son. The child died of exposure. {footnote 14} Without a doubt, many similar cases went unprosecuted and unrecorded. Folklore sources suggest that such fatal abuse of malformed children was not unusual.

The mistreatment of children in folklore accounts often (although not always) leads to a happy outcome for the human parents and their rightful child. To halt the abuse of their offspring, the otherworldly parents frequently rescue the child and return the stolen mortal child. Stories with these fantasy endings provided hope, wish fulfilment and escape to an era that was plagued with birth defects and debilitating infant diseases.

But not all changing accounts have happy endings. Often the child thought to be a changeling is driven away or killed, but there is no indication that the healthy original child is returned. The tales that omit the safe recovery of the rightful child authentically illustrate a painful aspect of family survival in pre-industrial Europe. A peasant family's very subsistence frequently depended upon the productive labour of each member, and it was enormously difficult to provide for a person who was a permanent drain on the family's scarce resources. The fact that the changelings' ravenous appetite is so frequently mentioned indicates that the parents of these unfortunate children saw in their continuing existence a threat to the sustenance of the entire family. Changeling tales support other historical evidence suggesting that infanticide was not infrequently the solution selected.

Brewing in eggshells

Cruel abuse is not the only way to force demonic parents into reclaiming their misshapen children in changeling legends, although this is the most frequently described method. A more humane approach was to force the changeling to laugh or to make him utter an expression of surprise, which, according to popular belief, would expose his true identity and force his supernatural parents to take him away. A common trick was to make preparations in the presence of the changeling to brew beer or to cook the stew in eggshells. This approach is described in some detail in Jacob Grimm's German Mythology {footnote 15} and is used in numerous folktales throughout Europe. Typically, the changeling responds with surprise, claiming that he is as old as a nearby forest but has never before witnessed such a sight.

The belief that a changeling was much older than the child he was impersonating could lead to a fear of the child, as illustrated in the Icelandic tale "The Changeling Who Stretched. This legend tells of a woman who is left alone in the house with a boy of confirmation age who is suspected of being a changeling. She watches in horror as the lad, who thinks that he is alone, yawns and stretches until he reaches the rafters. Terrified at being alone with this monster, the woman screams, and the boy collapses as if he had been shot, resumes his former size, and returns to his bed. It is easy to see how this tale could have grown out of a woman's fears of being left alone with a mentally retarded but sexually maturing male.

A changeling's ostensibly great age plays an important role in yet another folktale motif: the child who neither matures nor dies, remaining helplessly dependent and insatiably hungry for an interminable amount of time. The opening paragraph of the Norwegian tale

"The Changeling Betrays His Age"

exemplifies the problem: "On Lindheim Farm, in Nesherad, there was supposed to have been a changeling. No one could remember when he was born or when he had come to the farm. No one had ever heard him speak, but all the same, they were afraid to do anything to him or make him angry. He ate so much that the people at Lindheim had been living from hand to mouth, generation after generation, on his account."

Although other sources suggest that changelings seldom lived longer than seven years, or, at the longest, eighteen or nineteen years, {footnote 18} the fear could easily evolve that a changeling might survive several normal lifetimes, bringing poverty and suffering to a family for many generations. To some, the burden of caring for a retarded child must have appeared to be interminable. If one believed that such problems may not resolve themselves during an entire human lifetime, then drastic measures would be all the more justified.

Other protective measures
Changeling folklore not only explained why some children fail to grow and develop normally but also helped to justify the extreme actions that may have been taken (whether in fact or only in fantasy) to free the parents or society from the burden of caring for handicapped children; it also provided protective measures against demonic exchange.

The most frequently mentioned preventative practice, and one that undoubtedly evolved because of its positive consequences, was the insistence that the newborn infant be watched very carefully until certain danger periods had passed. "Women who have recently been delivered may not go to sleep until someone is watching over the child. Mothers who are overcome by sleep often have changelings laid in their cradles," recorded Jacob Grimm in his German Mythology. In the legend appropriately entitled "Watching Out for the Children," we are given to believe that a child would have been stolen by a supernatural being had not the parents been so watchful during the night. According to most beliefs, a newborn was to be watched continuously for the first three days of its life; a somewhat reduced but still high level of watchfulness was called for during the first six weeks. The fact that the mother (or her substitute) was expected to keep the baby close at hand for at least six weeks helped to protect it from environmental dangers aided the child's psychological development and contributed significantly to family cohesiveness.

Working mothers
An added benefit of the six weeks of close watching was the relief granted to the mother from some of her most strenuous duties, thus aiding her recovery from pregnancy and delivery. In "The Changeling in the Thuringian Forest," the infant exchange occurs when the mother leaves her baby alone in the house while she fetches wood, a common but strenuous household task. In other legends, {footnote 20} babies are

exchanged when landlords force peasant mothers to do difficult harvest labour before their six-week recovery periods are past. These accounts thus impart the lesson that women recovering from confinement should not do work that takes them away from their newborn babies. The last line of one such story states the lesson succinctly: "And from that time forth, he [the nobleman] resolved to never again force a woman who had recently given birth to work. not for the sake of the women but rather for the protection of their children. But, however stated, the mothers themselves shared in the benefits of this belief.

Although the welfare of the family (and of society at large) dictated that women recovering from childbirth be spared many of the strenuous tasks that normally were expected of them, the patriarchal bias of German society did not provide for a woman's workload to be lightened for her benefit. The only acceptable justification for this temporary relief from strenuous duties was the belief that the woman's child was thus being protected from supernatural harm. Numerous other superstitions regulating a woman's post-confinement activities confirm this view, for example, the belief that "if a woman spins wool, hemp, or flax within six weeks of her confinement, her child will someday be hanged." Consistent with changeling beliefs, this superstitious practice spared the recently delivered woman the hardest of the spinning tasks, not for her own sake but for the protection of her child.

Gender bias

Other aspects of changeling folklore illustrate this same

anti-female stance. Most changeling accounts deal with male babies, implying that the fairies, elves, trolls, and devils have but little use for a female human child. In fact, in some areas, boys were dressed in girls' clothing until they were ten or eleven years old to deceive supernatural kidnappers in search of young boys. Further, a number of the protective measures prescribed by tradition have a strong patriarchal bias. For example, the popular belief that "whenever the mother leaves the infant's room she should lay an article of the father's clothing on the child, so that it cannot be exchanged."

Organised religion

Numerous religion-oriented protective measures also evolved, which further strengthened the connection between changing beliefs and organised churches. {footnote 25} As one would expect, Catholics sought to shield infants with holy water, crucifixes, and representations of various saints, whereas Protestants relied on the Bible for protection, often placing the book itself (or perhaps a single page) in the crib as a talisman. In both faiths, the unbaptised child was deemed to be especially vulnerable, although baptism did not offer complete protection against demonic exchange. Interestingly, the Grimm brothers omit most references to Christianity in their writings on changelings, probably to emphasise their view that the changeling legends and practices still extant in nineteenth-century Germany were survivors from pre-Christian Europe.

The stolen child's perspective

Nearly all changeling tales are told from the concerned parents' point of view. In the same manner as the parents, we the audience learn that something is wrong with an infant, discover the cause, and are told how to effect a resolution. The perspective of another involved party—the changeling, the elf-parents, or the abducted child—is seldom represented. Shakespeare's A Midsummer Night's Dream builds an exception to this general rule. An important subplot of this play is built around Oberon's and Titania's (king and queen of the fairies) fight over the guardianship of a changeling boy. Another exception is found in the Finnish tale "The Kantele Player," {footnote 26}, in which we first learn that a child exchange has taken place when the abducted person—now a beautiful and mature woman—appears to a lonely young man who is playing a kantele (a Finnish harp) and reveals her story to him.

The couple seeks out the woman's father, a count, and convinces him that his supposed daughter, who is twenty-one years old and "will neither grow nor die," is in truth a changeling, a witch's daughter. "But what should we do with this child who has been with us for twenty-one years?" asks the count. Acting upon the advice of the returning daughter, who knows the ways of witches, they build a roaring fire, and the legitimate daughter herself throws the imposter into the flames. A cry is heard from the witches who have been watching through the window: "Don't burn our child!" The changeling's skin bursts from its body, and only an alder stump is left in the fireplace.

This story has a genuine fairytale ending (for everyone save the changeling). The kantele player, despite his poverty, marries the count's daughter, and -- we are told -- they still live in the stone house built for them by her grateful father.

Selma Lagerlöf
An even happier conclusion (this time for all parties concerned) is given to us by Selma Lagerlöf, who won the Nobel Prize for literature in 1909, in her children's book "The Changeling."} This artful fairy tale weaves the primitive motifs of troll lore into a humane and satisfying fantasy story. True to tradition, the author describes the kidnapping of a mortal child by an old troll woman, who leaves her misshapen baby in its place. Following the pattern of countless folk legends, the parents are told to beat the changeling child with a heavy cane if they want to recover their baby. The father is only too willing to abuse the ugly troll child, but the mother's maternal instincts cause her to intercede on the changeling's behalf. Several episodes are described, in which the father attempts to follow the community's expectations by cruelly punishing or even killing the unwanted child, but each time the mother selflessly protects the troll baby.

Her kindness and perseverance are rewarded in the end, and the two children are restored to their original parents. Only then do we learn that during his absence, the human child had lived in an unseen parallel world to that of his parents? Every act of cruelty or fondness visited upon the troll child by his human guardians had been duplicated upon him by his troll stepmother. It was a mother's kindness and humanity rather than the expected abuse and neglect that rescued her child. Lagerlöf thus cloaks an ancient and cruel superstition in a modern and humane dress.

Conclusion

The advance of science during the eighteenth and nineteenth centuries slowly but surely eroded the popular belief that malformed and retarded children likely were not human at all, but rather the offspring of some demonic being, offspring that could be neglected, abused, and even put to death with no moral compunctions. As these theological explanations for retardation gave way to medical explanations, community values and personal attitudes changed to such an extent that the very word "changeling," its synonym "kill crop," and their equivalents in other languages now have become historical. Curiosities, survivals of beliefs and practices that helped our northern European forebears—for good or for bad—face the problems of life and death when confronted with mentally or physically defective children The Elves," Jacob and Wilhelm Grimm, Children's and Household Tales (1812), no. 39/III; migratory legend type 5085. Translated by D. L. Ashliman. "A Changeling is Beaten with a Switch," Jacob and Wilhelm Grimm, German Legends (1816), no. 88; migratory legend type 5085. Translated by D. L. Ashliman. Other descriptions of changelings in the Grimms' German Legends are found in nos. 60, 82, 83, 89, 90, 91, and 153.

Printed in Great Britain
by Amazon